AF477284

from F*ck You Money to FIRE

enabling you to have enough money
to do what you think is important in your life
or not always or never again have to work

Merijn Heijnen

First international edition, November 2020

Hardcover ISBN 9789083105499
Paperback ISBN 9789083105451
E-book ISBN 9789083105444

https://fymfire.com/en

While all personal stories in this book are nothing but the truth, some names or details have been changed or omitted for reasons of confidentiality.

EN-HC-v1.2

The secret of happiness
is freedom.

And the secret of freedom
is courage.

Thucydides

Content

Part 0

Before we really get started

'A journey of a thousand miles begins with a single step'

Lao Tzu, Chinese philosopher and one of the founders of Taoism.

Foreword to the international edition

I have put a few months of my life into this book because of my need to share my ideas and to show that creating Fuck You Money (FYM) and achieving FIRE (Financially Independent Retire Early) is easier than you might think. I really hope and trust, that many people will be able to change their lifestyle so that they have more money for themselves, for beautiful things, for freedom and for financial independence.

This is the international edition. It is translated from my native language (Dutch) and some country specific details and examples have been removed. I have added some other country or more internationally relevant information. I have chosen to use the US dollar as the currency to exemplify and explain concepts and methods. In the examples it is not about the numbers but about the methods. Do not get distracted if you feel a specific number in an example is too high or too low. Think of the examples being in your own currency if needed. If your savings grow from 400 to 800 it does not matter if it's in euros, dollars, pounds or rupees. It's about the increase and the fact that the amount doubles.

I feel privileged that I was born where I was born and that I grew up in a safe environment and loving family. I am aware that not everyone gets the same opportunities. Everyone needs a bit of luck in their career and life. It is important to realize that you yourself are responsible for grabbing the opportunities that are offered to you.

I am thankful to Tracey, Wouter, Danny and Judith who helped me with their feedback on my manuscript, removing hundreds of commas and making it sound less foreign.

I am interested in how things can be improved and I appreciate your opinion, even (or especially!) if it is different from my own. Inaccuracies in the book, if any, are entirely my responsibility, and I would like to remove them for a next edition so please let me know. You can contact me via Facebook, Instagram or LinkedIn. You can also send me an email via merijn@fymfire.com.

Merijn Heijnen

Why I wrote this book

Many are struggling with their lives trying to fit into society and meet the demands they think are imposed on them. They are trying to live up to an ideal image of a successful father/mother, partner, friend, son/daughter, co-worker, entrepreneur and tax paying citizen.

I want to draw people's attention to the possibility of making a plan of their own, of making their own journey, of daring to be different, of daring to be smarter and of daring to make choices. I encourage (younger) people to start choosing for themselves earlier and to take care of themselves sooner. It is better to be sorry for having tried something than to be sorry for not having tried it.

I don't think retiring early is what everyone needs in their life. I do believe that there are moments in everyone's life you have to be able to say 'Fuck you, I will do that!' and then have money to pay for the consequences. Also, or especially, if the government or your employer doesn't provide for, or doesn't support, your decision.

When you become financially independent, you will no longer be dependent on a job, salary, government or family to provide for you. You become self-reliant and therefore have the opportunity to do something for yourself or give something back to the world.

I think if you make smarter, conscious choices you don't have to be stuck in a job you don't like. You don't have to burn yourself out to earn the amount of money you spend each month on things that, if you think about it, don't really matter.

It's my ambition to show everybody a simple approach that is easy to follow. I give a lot of attention to behavior, lifestyle choices and the fact that we let ourselves be influenced by others. I provide simple questions, answers, directions and tools to define your goals, to make your plan and to start a change in your life. I provide explanations of the things you need so you can immediately start saving and investing the money you don't spend.

Why you should read this book

The red pill and the blue pill in the film 'The Matrix' propose a choice between taking either a 'red pill' that reveals an unpleasant truth, or taking a 'blue pill' to remain in blissful ignorance. The red pill is described as the solution to find out the 'real truth' in life. Morpheus, a character in the film, explains that you have to dive into the famous 'rabbit hole' to learn about the lies of the world, so that you can break free of these lies and achieve freedom. The 'rabbit hole' we're talking about comes from the story 'Alice In Wonderland', where Alice literally falls into a rabbit hole and ends up in Wonderland.

Movie clip The Matrix - The blue pill or the Red pill. The link to this clip can be found at fymfire.com/en/notes/

In this book I present to you the red pill. Fuck You Money (FYM) is a way of thinking, as a tool, as an attitude and a means by which you can learn about the bullshit in the world that prevents you from achieving personal financial freedom (or 'wonderland'). You can do things with your life that matter to you. If you choose the red pill, you might choose to temporarily stop working or to stop working altogether. If you take the red pill I will show you that it is much easier than you think to create enough FYM and do the things you find important and want to do.

FYM is also literally the money you need to say 'Fuck You' to your boss, or your bank or your landlord. With FYM you can have a different attitude and relationship with people who think they hold power over you. From the moment you are no longer afraid of threats and pressure because you know you have enough FYM, you participate differently and you can put things into perspective.

Does your manager disagree? Fuck you! If you have decided that you need time for yourself, for something really important and this can't be done within your company's leave guidelines and sabbatical rules: 'Fuck You! This is simply the principle of FYM.

- What do you want for yourself, your family or your children?
- Why do you need FYM to achieve this?
- What is your dream?
- Why do you want to become more financially independent?
- Why do you want to retire early?

Buying your first property might be your dream but this is made difficult by government and financial institutions. You need enough FYM so you can enter the real estate market to buy your home anyway. Going on a bucket list trip around the world with your family might be your wish. You need enough FYM and there you go. Retiring early might be your ambition. You start building your FIRE capital, let it grow and make it happen.

Everybody has his or her own dreams, wishes and ambitions in life. Many people find it difficult to have the amount of money available at the moment it's needed to fulfil these dreams and wishes. This is Fuck You Money. Have enough money available to do what you want at the moment you desire, independent of an employer or government.

Who is this book for?

I am writing this book for my younger self, the person I was twenty-five years ago. If I can give my younger self a piece of advice, this would be it:

> *'Don't care too much about what others think of the choices you make. As soon as you make money, start keeping track of what you spend it on, and become aware of whether you think it's worth it. Don't compare yourself to others, neighbors or friends to see whether you have the same, more, better, nicer stuff but consider how you can handle your money smarter than them and save a larger part of your income. Put some of this money in your FYM jar and do the most fantastic things later on. Also keep some of your money separate and put it in your FIRE jar, which you invest smartly, so that you become more financially independent of a wage.'*

I am writing this book for anyone who, for whatever reason, does not always want to be dependent on a job, an employer or the government and who wants to decide for himself or herself what he or she spends money on.

I want this to be a book you can give to your partner. If, as you read this book, you agree a lot with what you read and find yourself nodding and thinking "Yes, that's what I think too" or "Yes, that's what I do" but you have the feeling that your partner needs a little nudge or information and inspiration, then this is your chance.

Fuck You Money for millennials (and generation Z)

For the young generation of working people, generation Y, the millennials, and the generation currently entering the labor market, generation Z, I find the creation of FYM more important than ever.

Some of these generations might have the notion that it is difficult for them to make ends meet with their money. They don't see how you can have a nice life and still not spend everything that comes in. Or how it is possible to save and build something for later. However, it is clear to these generations that they will be more responsible than previous generations for their own financial health, while it is unclear how things like pensions will work for them.

I want to tell these generations that you have all the time you need to work on your financial health. You are not yet (or not too much) bothered by the lifestyle creep in which you think that all kinds of luxury and perhaps superfluous things are essential to you. Many people of generation X seem to be in the middle of this and although they are used to make more money they easily spend it all, every month. My message is that creating Fuck You Money is more important than ever.

It seems more difficult for the current generations to earn enough income to be able to save enough to buy their own house and build up capital. Let alone to build up financial buffers, create Fuck You Money or think about the idea that you might not always want to work, or perhaps never work again. When you start working and making money it is quite challenging to get your life in order. Your income isn't very large yet and your expenses are growing faster, or at least as fast, as your income. And that's what it's all about.

Try to paint a more realistic picture of your desired lifestyle and the corresponding money behavior. When you were a student you probably went on vacation, with friends to a bar or to festivals. Now that you're making money, why can't you keep doing this? You can if you spend as much, or as little, money on it as you did when you were a student, and not suddenly two or three times as much, more often and for longer periods of time. You have acquired a number of responsibilities and expenses in this new phase of your life and you want to set aside money for all kinds of goals you never had to think about in your previous phase of life.

As a starter in this phase of life you actually have a number of advantages over older generations. First of all, you are aware of both the challenges and the opportunities early in your life, many people simply realize too late that they want to do something with money they don't have at that time. If you start saving right away, you can let your money grow for a longer period of time. You can start small and make a habit of 'just not spending all your money'.

Secondly, you already have more experience with flexible forms of working and living than the previous generation. You are less attached to old-fashioned, rigid, contracts and relationships with employers and the government. As generation X we think we need to own everything and above all we gather a lot of materialistic stuff in our lives. For millennials it's more possible to share things and more about having experiences instead of collecting things.

What this book is about

This book is about happiness, money, bullshit, Fuck You Money and FIRE. The book is especially about how to get more freedom in your life and inspiration about what you can do with it. This book is about getting a handle on your own life. Live life differently. I want to show how you can start with investing easily and cheaply even without understanding investment strategies. You will learn how insight into your spending pattern can lead to a change in lifestyle and escape the 'lifestyle creep'. It is about setting FIRE goals and choosing a direction of your journey. You can start now.

- This book is not about IRA, ISA or 401K. It is about YOU. It is about how you can easily start not spending all your money.
- This book is not about choosing the best ETF for you to reduce portfolio costs with an extra 0.1%. It is about changing behavior and choosing the best lifestyle for you to reduce your spending to a level that allows you to save and invest.
- This book is not about needing millions of dollars, pounds or euros to pay for a luxurious materialistic retired lifestyle. This book is about defining what you think is important in life and how much money you really need to achieve your goals.
- This book is not about reaching FIRE in your thirties after making 6 figure income and working yourself half dead for a few years. It is about understanding why you might want to work less or not at all and finding out when and how you can achieve this.
- This book is not about scaring you with financial terms, percentages and technically difficult things you need to do. It is about how you can easily start investing and set up your portfolio of low-cost diversified funds. It is about making small and fun steps so you can start directly.
- This book is not (really) about money. It is about better living by making smarter choices. In this book I want to show that freedom and independence can be bought with FYM.
- This book has no ambition to be about bullshit. Where this book is about bullshit, it is to show how to become smarter with brands, marketing and financial advice. And that if we can make authentic choices, it will result in less bullshit.

- This book is about insights from books and practical experience where I dare to say: the soft issue, often is the hard issue. The soft issues are the less tangible human issues – the attitudinal, cultural or mindset issues of people. Addressing the soft issues means talking and thinking about values, culture and behavior.
- This book is not (only) about FIRE (Financially Independent, Retire Early). Where this book is about FIRE, it is mainly meant for people who want to use the principles and insights of FIRE.

How this book is built up

Get, Keep, Grow, Achieve

Get, Keep, Grow and Achieve are four parts that together form your strategy to achieve your ambitions and realize your dream.

- Get - you somehow generate or earn money. It is interesting to explore if there are ways to increase your income now or in the future.
- Keep - you put a part of this income aside. You will save more money if you spend less. Someone who wants to become financially independent makes sure that he or she does not spend all the income that comes in. This can mean that you have to make smart choices about your lifestyle: where/how you are going to live, how you are going to transport yourself, entertain, feed yourself, and so on.
- Grow - you make good choices with the money you have left over. The unspent income you can invest somehow and by doing this you let your money grow. You deposit the money in a savings or deposit account, in investments or invested in a company, your own home, in several houses you rent out, or in relatively safe cheap widely spread ETF's (Exchange-Traded Funds) or index trackers.
- Achieve - once your FYM or FIRE jar is sufficient and FI (Financial Independence) has been achieved, you can decide to finance the choices you make in your life from this. You have reached your goal. You have enough FYM which can be either a well-stocked bucket list jar or a situation where you are completely financially independent to retire early. Achieve is about celebrating that you have achieved this but also about replanning and recalibrating everything.

Why, What, How

The main reason I have divided this book into three parts 'Why', 'What' and 'How' is because the importance of a beautiful dream, a good ambition or a clear vision is often underestimated. We are inclined to step directly into the 'How', to start acting immediately, full of devotion but often with a lot of trial and error and sometimes completely in the wrong direction. By first paying attention to the 'Why' and then the 'What' I want to prevent you from making a false start at the beginning of your journey by going straight into the 'How'.

Why

Why is all about dreams and ambitions. You can't reach a goal without a vision and you can't climb a mountain without ambition. You can't change your lifestyle or your own behavior without making your aim clear to yourself.

- Becoming aware of the 'Why': formulate your dream and answer the questions 'Why do you want to create FYM? What do you want to do with your FYM? Why do you aspire FIRE?'
- Become aware of what money is currently coming in, what is going out and why there isn't enough left over.
- Dreams and inspiration about 'Get', 'Keep', 'Grow', 'Achieve'.

What

You can't build a house without a design and you can't develop a website without a framework. You can't start making changes to your life without being clear on what choices and decisions to make.

- Designing a lifestyle that suits you and your ambitions. Plan how to adapt your behavior to your desired lifestyle, come up with ideas on how to save money.
- How much money do you want, when do you want to stop working, how long do you want to stop working and what do you want to be able to do?
- Formulating Get, Keep, Grow & Achieve ambitions and making plans based on these ambitions.

How

Finally, you can't build an airplane in the sky and you can't start building the roof of a house before the foundation is solid. You can't just start doing all the actions and expect to save a lot of money right away. This requires some organization. You can achieve your ambitions by cutting them up up into smaller manageable goals and tasks, through experimenting, evaluating and changing your course when necessary.

- What will your new lifestyle be like? Can you increase your income stream? Experiment with consuming less or in a different way and unlearning habits in order to save money. Start investing, learn, evaluate and adapt.
- How do you manage and monitor your (passive) income?
- How do you redesign your lifestyle?

How to use (read) this book and online resources

I Aspire to make the somewhat inaccessible and sometimes complex subjects of Fuck You Money and FIRE easier to handle and comprehend. I will do this by explaining what I think a FYM journey can look like and by talking you through the phases 'Why', 'What' and 'How'. I will explain how you can design and execute four basic strategies 'Get', 'Keep', 'Grow' and 'Achieve' to create FYM and achieve Financial Independence (FI) and/or to retire early (RE).

'The soft issue is often the hard issue', this is an insight I regularly have had in my work as a management consultant and when working with teams. Every time it turns out that even with the 'hardest' changes in an organization, such as information technology, financial systems or cost reduction, culture and behavior are the most difficult to actually change. People want to change but don't want to be changed. Changing behavior is difficult, takes time and only works if it is clear why change is necessary. The person needs to understand the importance of the change, feel the urgency and see the benefits.

This is also how it works with FYM and FIRE. Practical matters such as opening an investment account and determining an investment strategy may not be so difficult for you. Adjusting your own behavior in such a way that you have money left over is probably more difficult. You are probably aware of this. Use the concepts, ideas and tools I offer you in this book. Be patient with yourself.

If you are interested in the practical side of creating FYM and achieving FIRE, I advise you to browse through the book and first skip some parts. You do not have to read this book linearly from cover to cover. If you are already convinced that you want to go for it and take a few first steps as soon as possible, you can go to 'Part 3: How'. When you have completed your first actions it might be useful to go back to the Why and What and read the first two parts for inspiration.

In this book I refer to books, articles, podcasts and videos. As a (free) resource with this book I've made online notes that you can use next to this book to easily find the things that interest you. I have indicated with icons that the relevant information and tools can be found on the online notes page. I recommend that you keep the online notes page opened for you to look at the relevant information whilst reading the associated part in the book. You can find the notes at fymfire.com/en/notes/. On fymfire.com/en/tools/ you can find (freely available) sample worksheets that I have made and find useful.

For further deepening your knowledge or understanding and for discussions about relevant topics I refer to: https://www.reddit.com/r/financialindependence/. I certainly don't think nor pretend that I personally hold all the necessary wisdom, and it is on this platform that you can see different opinions or get reactions from like-minded people. There is not only one correct answer to most questions and there is not usually one best choice. The diversity of the members guarantees that you will be further inspired and have more information so that you can make your own choices and decisions.

You can find the notes at www.fymfire.com/en/notes/

On www.fymfire.com/en/tools/ you can find examples of worksheets I've made and find useful.

For further information and discussion, I refer to www.reddit.com/r/financialindependence/ (810k Members, November 2020).

What else do you need?

- A notebook or notes app - for capturing ideas.
- A To Do list or a To Do app - for formulating, capturing and managing your actions.
- A calculator or a spreadsheet, such as Microsoft Excel or Google Sheets (online) - for playing with numbers, analyzing your expenses, keeping track of budgets and calculating to what extent you reach your goals.

The small print

Just to be clear: besides this book, I sell nothing; no training, no online coaching program, no financial advice. In this book I answer a lot of questions that I have been asked so many times in my life and I share the insights that I have gained in my work and non-work life.

I don't write pieces to promote any company, product or service. I don't recommend a particular bank, broker, stock, fund or anything else, and I don't make money with it.

I use the https://fymfire.com/en/ website to give you easy access to things I find inspiring, such as blogs, articles, podcasts and videos. I don't add anything that I find irrelevant or that I don't fully support.

I encourage you to borrow the books I recommend from the library or buy and read them. It does not cost you anything extra if you buy a book I endorse via for example an Amazon link.

Try things out before you conclude whether or not it is something for you. People have different preferences and ways of working.

This book is meant to help you in your journey to Fuck You Money and Financial Independence and to help you realize your ambitions and dreams. The information presented is for informational purposes only. This book contains the author's opinions and ideas. It is intended to be inspiring and to offer useful material on the topics covered.

Part 1

Why

'Too many people spend money they haven't earned to buy things they don't want to impress people that they don't like.'

Will Rogers, often quoted famous American actor and writer.

Chapter 1
Why Fuck You Money

Why Fuck You Money for everyone?

Many people think that certain things that cost a lot of money, such as owning a home or the education of their children, cannot be paid for without the help of an employer, the government or a loan from a financial institution. Many people don't give serious thought to not working for a long period of time. They might think it's not for them or that it's not feasible. Many people are somewhat dependent on an employer or the government when it comes to providing income, both now and in the future.

I believe that it is possible for almost everyone with an income to create FYM. For almost everyone there will come a time when FYM can offer some form of financial independence in life. Having FYM can mean that someone can bring in their own money for a mortgage deposit. It can mean that someone can let his or her child study and live on his or her own. Or it means that someone chooses to work less or not to do any paid work at all.

Everyone in his or her life can apply the ideas and approaches from this book and thus free up a part of his or her disposable income and let it grow. I believe that everyone can be a little more creative, not give so much thought to what others think and make conscious and intentional choices. You don't have to lack anything or compromise on the quality of the things that are important to you.

I am happy and time-rich but not really rich in the financial sense of the word. My net worth is somewhere around the average or median in the Netherlands. However, I have made choices in my life that have resulted in some capital and passive income which in combination with very low spending levels allows me not to need to do any paid work. I concern myself only with what I want and what makes me and my wife happy, independent of income from work or any contribution from the government.

It seems to be an inevitable trend that we have to contribute more ourselves and become more personally responsible for financing our retirement. There may be an endless list of possible reasons for you personally to want something in the future that doesn't suit your employer and for which your employer or government isn't willing to pay.

- The time and money to make a bucket list trip with your partner or family
- The time and money to care for your child or your parents
- A college fund for your child so no student loan is needed
- The time and money for mid-career study
- The money to make a down payment to start your home loan
- The time and money to quit your job and start working for yourself
- The time and money to not work for a year and renew your energy
- To not have to work for money from a certain age
- … ?

While for many people it is an uncomfortable idea to detach themselves from an employer or government that transfers a monthly amount to the bank account, it can be very liberating to put this fear aside for a while. It may well be that you are far better able to finance certain choices you want to make in your life than you realize. You may very well be able to take care of financing an extra study later in life, for retraining to become something you feel good about, for extended parental leave, for a family sabbatical 'in between jobs', for a long sabbatical to travel around the world or for retiring early. For this you need Fuck You Money.

The rat race

How Dave in his hamster wheel life runs a rat race with his lifestyle creep and bullshit job because he doesn't have Fuck You Money.

Imagine Dave. Dave has neatly completed his education, has the right diplomas in his pocket and has long since paid off his student debt. He works in a laboratory for a large successful company in FMCG (Fast Moving Consumer Goods). The company tries to sell consumers as many consumer products as possible ranging from ice creams to cooking oils and from detergent to body lotion.

Dave's job is to invent and find ingredients that will allow the company to legally make a claim that it's good for something. Dave researches the properties of the craziest additions to, for example, shampoo, like vanilla and cucumber or sheep's wool and flower oil.

Dave works pretty hard, there's a lot going on but gradually he finds out that this is absolutely not what he thought he had studied for. Dave lacks a sense of purpose and meaning because he has the feeling that he is only fooling people. He doesn't feel appreciated and apart from the salary he needs to pay the high mortgage there is nothing that makes him get out of bed and into work every morning. Dave realizes that he is stuck in a bullshit job.

Dave can't leave the job; he needs the income and has a career that many people dream of at a well-known company with good terms of employment. He got a promotion and there is now the word manager on his business card. This means that he manages a number of colleagues. With this new job only comes more bullshit: more meetings, nonsensical administrative work and longer working days.

'How long can I keep this up?' Dave thinks to himself. 'How long do I actually have before retirement?'

Dave bought a new house not so long ago. He saw that with his salary and the increase in value of the house where they lived, he could get a much higher mortgage, buy a bigger and more luxurious house and even live in a better neighborhood. Dave saw that even with the favorable conditions this meant a considerable increase in the monthly costs but he didn't care; 'I can pay it' and 'I work hard for it'.

Dave also has a great new car and he always orders the newest iPhone at the very moment Apple comes up with a new model. The iPhones in the family are passed on, Dave's partner now has the previous model and also the youngest kid has a fairly recent iPhone model.

They completely replaced the kitchen in their new house. Although it all worked fine, it was clearly a few years old. Some of the old kitchen appliances did not have the latest gadgets and features that Dave's friends, neighbors and family all have in their kitchen nowadays.

They prefer not to spend too much time preparing an evening meal, because everyone is at home at a different time. It really comes in handy that the ready-to-eat meal can be heated in the microwave. They prefer to go out to dinner with the whole family if they want some family time.

They don't dine in the greatest restaurants but it's nice and convenient. The package vacations are booked and paid for. The vacations are not to dream destinations but arenice for the kids and again convenient because you don't have to arrange anything. After all, it is a vacation.

All the cell phone subscriptions, TV, unlimited internet, on-demand music, film and sports packages make a big monthly dent in the budget. The cars, phones, vacations, subscriptions, hobbies, eating out; it all costs a lot of money, on top of the high monthly mortgage costs. Dave can pay for it all but he doesn't have anything left at the end of the month.

Dave sometimes wonders whether there's another way but he's stuck with his bullshit job because of the lifestyle creep. Dave is so used to all the things that he spends money on in his life they have become essential. In fact, it seems to him that he's entitled to all the luxury he can afford. Here's the hamster wheel that Dave can't possibly get out of without a big change. He's done exactly what society expects of him and he lives neatly by the rules of our consumer marketing driven culture. He realizes that he only works to pay for this lifestyle. He also thinks he has no choice but to continue working for the next thirty years, hopefully to be eligible for early retirement, or maybe he can get out of it in case of a major reorganization, with a nice severance scheme.

Dave's example serves to show that a life without FYM that seems perfect on the outside is in reality not always without its problems underneath.

During this period in many people's lives people are confronted with labor disputes, relationship problems, health problems, extramarital affairs, burn-outs, depression, midlife crises and combinations of these problems. This is a moment in many people's lives they had wished they had FYM at their disposal.

This is the moment in the lives of some where FYM is used for a career switch, or a family-gap-year, or a mini-retirement, or a world trip 'in-between-jobs' or just financial free time to catch their breath.

This is a moment in your life when you want to be financially independent enough to make important choices without being dependent on an employer, manager, or government.

Making choices in your life

Nobody knows how life will work out, what obstacles you will meet and what possibilities may come your way. If you have enough FYM it will be much easier for you to solve problems, navigate around obstacles and embrace opportunities. You can say, “Fuck You” to things that hinder or slow you down and say, “Hell Yeah!” to possibilities, great opportunities and fun things.

Steve Jobs gave a speech to graduating students at Stanford University in 2005 with beautiful, powerful and wise words. He talks about 'dropping out' of the system, and 'dropping in' in what you like and what you choose. He talks about karma, gut feeling, destiny, leaving the beaten path and doing what you love.

> *"You got to find what you love and love what you do, don't settle. Remembering every day that you are going to die, is the best way to avoid the trap of thinking you have something to lose. There is no reason not to follow your heart. Your time is limited, so don't waste it living someone else's life. Don't let the noise of others' opinions drown out your own inner voice."*

Steve addresses the graduating students in the speech with what he has always wished for himself.

> *"Stay hungry. Stay foolish."*

Steve Jobs 2005 Stanford Commencement Address

A life with FYM is a life in which you have decided not to spend all of the money coming in; you put an amount aside every month. It is a life where you have decided not to be unnecessarily seduced by consumerism; you don't buy more than you need. It is a life in which you value time and quality, you make your own choices about what you do with whom and what you spend your precious time and money on. It is a life in which you let yourself be guided by wishes and dreams rather than by fears and uncertainties. You have said goodbye to the eternal fear of missing something (Fear Of Missing Out) and you are not insecure about what other people think of you when you deviate from the mainstream. It's a life in which you're not stuck in the rat race, you're not bothered by 'lifestyle creep'. It is a life in which you are in the driver’s seat, you decide which direction it takes, you make your own choices.

Chapter 2
Why less bullshit

Bullshit and bullshit jobs

Before I continue and frequently use the word Bullshit (BS), I would like to briefly explain why I find it necessary to use this word and what I want to make clear with it. When I read the book 'Bullshit jobs' by David Graeber, an anthropologist, I recognized many of the descriptions of people and jobs, companies and managers, problems and situations. In my work I have come to know and seen many companies from the inside and I find it aptly described how some people are aware of the futility of their jobs and yet continue with their daily drudge. What is emphasized in the book is that a job is only a bullshit job if the employee (also) perceives it that way. A bullshit job is not a denigrating term; it is not looked down upon by others, only by yourself. You can't say a job is a bullshit job if the employee enjoys it or finds the work meaningful. It is up to you to decide whether or not you have a (partial) bullshit job. And whether or not to do something about it.

David Graeber, Bullshit Jobs:
The Rise of Pointless Work, and What We Can Do About It

I also use the word bullshit in this book for many other things than a job. While reading the book Bullshit Jobs I had to think about how many of the things we buy in our lives are to a large extent bullshit. But what I mean by this is that I think it's bullshit myself and that can of course be very different for someone else. What if I don't find something BS at all? What if I just need a little BS sometimes? BS is often just fun, nice or easy. Many products with a high BS factor are relatively expensive and that's what you'll have to realize in the context of this book. These are products where so much money is spent on marketing that you hardly pay for the product. As with bullshit jobs, it's up to you to see if something is bullshit for you and what you want to do with it.

Bullshit paradise

We live in bullshit paradise. I get frustrated by some of the claims made by famous brands that charge a higher price for, a sometimes, inferior product. It shows a lack of respect for me as a consumer by the marketeers and sellers of those products. We are made to believe that the product has some functional benefits, when in reality it does not include enough or anything at all to actually offer the claimed benefits to the customer/consumer.

To make sure that you do taste or notice something, all kinds of other ingredients are added which are mostly cheap, usually not healthy, often artificial and sometimes downright fake. A lot of effort is put into coloring margarine to make it look like butter, and into artificially modified proteins that have taken over the properties of vanilla so that custard and ice cream taste like vanilla. Think about the insane ingredients that are used to color, scent or flavor your yogurt drink pink or to color light bread dark so it looks healthy, or to give it the flair of being traditionally baked! We're not stupid, or are we?

I don't want to start a crusade against producers and stores that see the above as a good business model. I just want to make you think smarter about what you're buying and then adapt your behavior to choose a lifestyle that you can safely call 'conscious'. Conscious, because you think about things before you do them, because you think about your need before you buy something, you think about the added value for you, because you are the only one here who makes the choices and decisions about spending your money. If you take the decision overnight that from then on you will think smarter about what your real needs are, you automatically end up with money to spare at the end of the month. You can reconsider whether it really should be the newest and most comprehensive model of product X to fulfil your need. You can let go of what unrealistic fantasy the brand builders are trying to present to you. Not constantly taking into account what others think of you liberates you from the shackles of consumerism. This is the beginning of your FYM or FIRE money to use for beautiful and important things in your life.

Salt scooped out of the Mediterranean waters around Ibiza using traditional methods? Or Celtic salt? Or pink Himalayan salt? Or kosher natural, handcrafted, gourmet, pyramid sea salt flakes? Manually harvested during summer eco-friendly sustainable salt from the ancient underground dried up rivers in some far away desert? Or fleur de sel, the 'flower of salt', harvested manually in the right weather conditions in a unique nature reserve with hundreds of flowers and birds (and I'm not making this up!)?

All the salt is pretty much the same, it's all ancient, it all dried up once, it all tastes salty. The most expensive salt at an ordinary supermarket costs around US$32 per kilogram, the cheapest at the same US$0.49 per kilogram. I found salt with herbs, flowers and seeds that sells for around US$100 per kg. Why on earth would you pay more for salt than for smoked salmon or a magnificent steak?

Less stuff

Many books have been written about minimalism and decluttering. I'm not a minimalist but I've benefited a lot from decluttering my life in different steps. The happiest people don't have the best of everything, they just make the best of everything. The importance of reducing the amount of stuff in your life lies in a number of things.

First: Immediately stop buying bullshit stuff.
Right away. Right now. Never buy anything without thinking about it first. From now on you give yourself time to think. You only buy something that really gives you value or function and not because it's on sale or because you get three of them for the price of two, and you really only need one. Buy less, buy less bullshit stuff, create more FYM.

Second: Lose your Fear Of Missing Out (FOMO) and Fear Of Better Options (FOBO).
You can immediately stop comparing yourself to others. You can stop buying things because you think it’s expected of you or because everyone else around you has one. Give yourself time to think about it. Think about why you want something and what function you are looking for it to fill and then think about which option fits your wish list perfectly.

Third: Avoid ending up in a 'lifestyle creep' in which you think that all kinds of luxury and perhaps superfluous things are essential to you.
Leave the thought behind that you have a right to have something, that you deserve it or that you work so hard for it. Just don't do it. Don't end up in this unnecessary dependence so you don't have to break with it later. Less luxury and superfluous stuff, no 'lifestyle creep', more FYM.

Fourth: Own less stuff and you need less storage space.
You can have a smaller house; you pay less rent or mortgage and you can create more FYM.

FOMO FOBO

Most people find it difficult to overcome fear and insecurity. I also realize that you learn to deal better with fear and insecurity better when you get older. In a society where we are constantly aware of what others do, how they do it, how they look, what they wear, what they buy, what they promote, what they like, it is hard to remain yourself. It is difficult not to let yourself be influenced in such a way that you feel miserable because you think you can't live up to what you see others have or do.

Fear Of Missing Out often has to do with a strong desire for social acceptance among peers. Young adults in particular can jeopardize their priorities and identity just to 'belong'.

Fear Of Better Options makes you indecisive, you don't see what the best option is. You can feel sorry afterwards, because you still doubt whether you have chosen the best option. It can make you really unhappy.

Things like FOMO and FOBO are driven by uncertainty and you can do something about it. You can choose to not constantly compare yourself with others and you can choose to not constantly doubt whether what you do, buy or make is the best. Just good is good enough.

JOMO

JOMO (Joy of Missing Out) is your antidote to FOMO. It is essentially about being satisfied with where you are in life. Give yourself some JOMO.

Deal with your time consciously: plan things that are important to you, whether it's sports, meeting a friend for coffee, writing that book or completing a work project. Make your time your priority instead of wasting time worrying about what other people are doing or thinking.

Embrace tech-free time: Log out of social media accounts and unfriend people who trigger your FOMO or cause you any kind of negativity. Set limits on how long you can spend on social media or remove certain social media apps from your phone.

Practice saying 'No': you don't always have to go everywhere, participate in everything, respond to messages or take that call.

Experience real life (not life on social media). The time you free up by not scrolling through feeds on social media can be spent on the things you like and care about, such as cooking, spending time away from home and spending time with your friends and family.

Slow down and take time to think before you say anything. Take the time to get somewhere for example by walking and notice that you see more. Take the time to do something with awareness and intent, and notice that you can enjoy it more.

Less bullshit in your life?

Call it minimalism, essentialism, simplism, functionalism or just less bullshit. Before making a purchase, think about what the most important function is for you, why do you want to buy it in the first place? If you don't have a good answer to this question, you might be less inclined to actually buy it.

If you have been able to answer this question to your satisfaction, go a level deeper, ask yourself which functions are important for the purpose you want to use it for. Draw up a list of specifications. Consider what is a 'must', what is 'important', what is 'nice to have' and what is 'unimportant'. Include this list in your online search and see which types and models meet the most important wishes and requirements. See if there's a big price difference between older models that can do the same and newer models that can do the same plus all kinds of things that are not important to you. Look for the bullshit factor with this product, which features make this product extra expensive without adding anything for you?

You should know that almost every major producer of consumer products makes different versions of the same product, for different customers (e.g. supermarkets) and different brands. Sometimes the different products have a slightly different recipe and of course a different packaging and brand promise.

Check the number of different types of milk in your supermarket. Depending on where you live half to all of the milk on the shelf, including various special types of milk, such as the expensive Meadow Fresh milk, comes from the same factory. All milk in all those different packages even comes from the same tanks. It is 100% the same milk! The only difference besides the packaging is the price. Bullshit!

This applies to many so-called white-label products, which are made by a factory that usually also makes branded products. More or less the same products are produced for different brands. This goes for most of the products you buy in the supermarket and at the drugstore but also for the more expensive things in life, from a bike to a car. We are so influenced by others, friends, vague acquaintances, even strangers, neighbors and marketeers that it seems as if we don't (dare to) have an opinion ourselves, don't (dare to) understand anything and don't (dare to) make our own choices.

Good coffee is important to me. During my travels I have visited many coffee plantations in Central and South America, in Africa and in South and Southeast Asia. I learned a lot there and this has influenced my view and opinion about good coffee.

Everything you've ever wanted to know about coffee

In Tanzania, for example, almost all the beans grown by farmers in the area on and around Mount Kilimanjaro are sold through a cooperative and a coffee auction. Different levels of quality have been determined based on the shape and size of the selected beans. It is absolutely true that a certain AA selection of beans from a certain crop of a certain plantation may be of better quality than any other selection. Unfortunately, this is not reflected in the coffee or even the loose beans you buy at a large supermarket, even though it says so on the packaging Single Origin Tanzania. This producer buys big and throws all the beans together.

Can we agree that for a toffee frappuccino with whipped cream, it doesn't matter at all whether it contains Single Origin coffee from some exotic country or not? For this heavily overpriced cup with mainly sugar and fat, the bullshit factor is very high. You can easily remove this from your routine and if you want to buy a real coffee at Starbucks, let's see what a Pikes Place drip coffee costs.

I want to clear up a possible misunderstanding immediately. I think Starbucks uses great coffee beans. I've been to a (roasting) factory and I've visited a plantation in Panama where some of the Starbucks beans come from. I believe Starbucks buys the best quality coffee beans and achieves the best price for itself as well as the coffee farmers and merchants. You can enjoy this for the paltry sum of around US$2.15 if you don't let the marketeers or one of the hip baristas influence you in buying the bullshit products for far too high a price.

Less Bullshit

- Less BS, because you know you don't need more stuff
- Less BS, because you don't need a newer, flatter, bigger, nicer, lighter, stronger ... every time
- Less BS, because you know that all the new stuff in your life after a short period of bliss just turns out to be more junk
- Less BS, because you have managed to wriggle yourself out of heavy consumerism
- Less BS, because you decide if, when and how much you want from something

Chapter 3
Why FIRE

From Fuck You Money to FIRE

Fuck You Money is for everyone. FIRE, becoming fully financially independent and quitting paid work early, is not the ultimate goal for everyone. Some people need millions of dollars to be able to quit their job and continue their life and lifestyle. Some people need a few hundred thousand to not have a paid job and life a happy life.

In my thinking about FIRE I was influenced by the early death of my father from cancer. Luckily, he had been able to retire a few years early and he and my mother enjoyed some years of freedom, independence, travel, a lot of fun and a lot of leisure. But not enough. It suddenly became clear to me that a lot of people don't get very old at all. A large number of the people who have worked all their lives and built up a decent pension will never be able to enjoy it, because life is finite. The discomforts of old age, sometimes life-threatening diseases and sub-optimal mental health for many prevent the enjoyment of retirement in good health. Unfortunately life has its own agenda. Life doesn't always allow a decline in health to start only after you have been able to do everything you always wanted to do.

During the period of the illness and ultimately the death of my father, I decided once and for all not to wait too long. Not to postpone too much. Not to focus my whole life on reaching retirement at the age of 66 (this is the current retirement age in the Netherlands but this is slowly going up). My motto has always been that I would rather regret something I try than regret something I didn't do.

In my thinking about FIRE I am influenced by my travels. If you apply geo-arbitrage (I'll elaborate on that later) to the maximum you will see that you have a lot more spending power with your money earned in a country like the Netherlands, the US or the UK if you take it elsewhere. Life is good in a country like the Netherlands but it's also costly. There are only around twelve countries in the world where the total cost of living (COL) is higher than in the Netherlands. This means that it is cheaper in about 90% of the countries in the world and if you live in the capital Amsterdam you score even worse. The difference between the COL in different countries is huge. This means that it is cheaper for me to travel across the world than to live in the Netherlands.

How has this affected my thinking about FIRE? Thinking smarter about what you really need and how to spend accordingly brings FI and even retiring early within reach for people who see FIRE as unattainable in their lives. It becomes easier to accumulate sufficient capital to finance such a life, and from then on you never have to work again. Believe me it is possible to pay for a simple but comfortable life for about US$1,000 a month. A quick calculation results in the required capital of US$300,000 or a passive income of US$12,000 a year. That is also FIRE. If you want or need to fit in your FIRE plan the costs of expensive college for your kids or expensive healthcare for yourself this will change your calculation considerably.

The fisherman and the businessman
(Paolo Coelho)

There was once a businessman who was sitting by the beach in a small Brazilian village. As he sat, he saw a Brazilian fisherman rowing a small boat towards the shore having caught quite a few big fish. The businessman was impressed and asked the fisherman, 'How long does it take you to catch so many fish?'

The fisherman replied, 'Oh, just a short while.'

'Then why don't you stay longer at sea and catch even more?' The businessman was astonished.

'This is enough to feed my whole family,' the fisherman said.

The businessman then asked, 'So, what do you do for the rest of the day?'

The fisherman replied, 'Well, I usually wake up early in the morning, go out to sea and catch a few fish, then go back and play with my kids. In the afternoon, I take a nap with my wife, and evening comes, I join my buddies in the village for a drink - we play guitar, sing and dance throughout the night.'

The businessman offered a suggestion to the fisherman: 'I am a PhD in business management. I could help you to become a more successful person. From now on, you should spend more time at sea and try to catch as many fish as possible. When you have saved enough money, you could buy a bigger boat and catch even more fish. Soon you will be able to afford to buy more boats, set up your own company, your own production plant for canned food and distribution network. By then, you will have moved out of this village to Sao Paulo, where you can set up HQ to manage your other branches.'

The fisherman continues, 'And after that?'

The businessman laughs heartily, 'After that, you can live like a king in your own house, and when the time is right, you can go public and float your shares in the Stock Exchange, and you will be rich.'

The fisherman asks, 'And after that?'

The businessman says, 'After that, you can finally retire, you can move to a house by the fishing village, wake up early in the morning, catch a few fish, then return home to play with kids, have a nice afternoon nap with your wife, and when evening comes, you can join your buddies for a drink, play the guitar, sing and dance throughout the night!'

The fisherman was puzzled, 'Isn't that what I am doing now?'

It doesn't matter if you are on your way to independently do the things you want during your (working) life, or if you are on your way to never having to work again after a certain moment. Everything that goes for one also goes for the other. It starts with designing and setting up a lifestyle that doesn't cost too much money, then depositing the money you have left into your FYM, bucket list or FIRE account and investing it so that the money grows and generates passive income.

To me the most important thing about both the FYM and the FIRE lifestyle is the actual choice of a lifestyle based on attention, intention, making your own choices, learning the rules of the game and playing the game just as smart to achieve the ultimate freedom you want.

Live differently

You don't always have to work full-time, all year round, every year until you reach retirement age. You can also work part of the year and the other part of the year you don't. You can work one year and not work another. You can also work for years and then not work for a full year every five years.

The time you don't work you can spend as you want, with whom you want and where you want. You can take care of your children or your parents. You can paint or write or play music for a year. You can travel or live in another country. You can work as a volunteer, in your own country or somewhere else.

We met Brian and Laura in one of the Seven Sister States in Northeast India. They live and work in Australia for one year and then travel for one year, mainly in Asia. Every 'working year' they live wherever they find work. They are very flexible and take advantage of regional differences in the labor market and the housing market. He is a driver and she is a teacher. They earn two normal salaries for one year and they only spend one salary. Every working year they save enough in Australian dollars to travel comfortably for a full year in the Asian countries. They have been doing this for 26 years!

We met Jenna and Matt in Ecuador. They live in Canada and have been working as teachers for five years. During these five years they save more than enough to travel for a year and do everything on their bucket list. They explained to us that more Canadians set up their lives in this X over Y way (X/Y). With the X/Y leave you can take different numbers of years off. For example, work four years and take the fifth free (4 over 5). And yes, Matt has already applied for his next X over Y.

What is X/Y not?
Two travelling Canadians, a ukulele, a cat & a hammock

Financially it is much easier to organize than you think, I'll explain how in this book. For now, I'll give a brief example. This is a simplified example where life events like having a partner or children and factors like inflation aren't taken into account.

X/Y example scenario

John, 30 years old, earns a net disposable income of US$2400 per month. After reading this book he decided the following: work for 5 years, followed by 1 year not working and repeat this a number of times.

During his financially free years in which he does not work he wants to live in different places in the world. He would like to learn Spanish, do volunteer work, relax and gain energy and inspiration for the next five years working back in his home country. He finds out how he can keep repeating this until he retires at the age of 69 at the latest.

He decides not to spend 20% of his disposable income, half of which goes into a FYM account and the other half into a FIRE account. From the FYM he pays his financially free year. He keeps this money without risk on a savings account and he hardly gets any return on it. The FIRE account is an investment account. He consistently deposits the amount every month and invests it in low-cost, well-spread index trackers.

During his financially free years, he spends just over US$1200 per month x 12 months, or about US$14,000 per year in countries where the cost of living is generally low.

His 36th, 41st, 47th and 53rd years he does not work, he learns Spanish in Quito, learns to surf in Bali, does nothing at all in southern Italy and spends a year volunteering somewhere in Africa.

At the age of 59 he takes stock and despite the years of not working and spending all his FYM, his FIRE account has almost US$155,000. Withdrawing from his FIRE account and spending about US$1580 a month on cost of living John can now decide to live somewhere in the world for the last 10 years until his retirement age. He will then never have to work again. Or he stays in his home country and takes it easy for the last 10 years. He will look for a stress-free job, with which he earns enough to pay for his cost of living until his retirement age, supplemented with his monthly FIRE amount. This is a different approach to how to live differently.

For the financial details of this example go online to 'Tools'.
on fymfire.com/en/tools/

My story from Fuck You Money to FIRE

From the moment I started making money (1999) I immediately started creating Fuck You Money. I started to explain the concept and my experience to friends. Some people picked up on it, others thought I had gone crazy.

Travel

During my studies I went on a long trip to Central America of about twelve weeks. After graduating I went on a trip to South America for four months. Immediately after my trip I started working, without a penny in my bank account and a (not shockingly high) student debt.

Work (in employment)

My first job was at a large well-organized company where I got the keys to my first lease car on the first day. International introduction weeks and training sessions were a great start to a promising career.

My department was all about Management, Control & Finance. Like my colleagues and customers I wore a suit and gray was the dominant color. The problems we had to solve were interesting for my colleagues but I noticed that I was more attracted to what colleagues in other departments were doing. It became clear to me what my future career would behold in the MC&F department. It could be neatly mapped out from beginning to ending up with a Financial Director position at a large company. The future was bright indeed but all was neatly colored within the lines, every step predictable and accompanied by utterly boring training. I soon decided that this was not for me.

Very different direction, work hard play hard

I kept working at the same company but in a department where it was all about Creativity, Innovation, Strategy & Collaboration. There weren't just men working, the suits weren't just gray and my colleagues and clients were diverse in terms of background and interests. It was much more fun. I started a totally uncertain career which was discouraged by the more serious people around me and I loved it. I started as a junior but I got opportunities, I learned a lot and worked hard.

It was a comfortable life I was living in Amsterdam from where I drove my lease car to the office or a customer somewhere in the country every day. I worked absurd hours (very regularly >100 hours a week) and during some periods I more often slept in a hotel next to the office than in my own bed at home. But I loved it. Working with an enthusiastic team of professionals on complex issues and solving them with creativity and innovation was great. I didn't suffer from stress but my colleagues and I struggled a bit with the tenability of such a high-pressure situation.

My FYM account grew steadily. I put money aside every month.

Short sabbatical, travel and divemaster training

After a couple of years I realized that there were a few things that I didn't get around to in my life. I wanted to become a divemaster (DM). I had done the Rescue Diver training in my limited evening hours. Combining the DM training with my work schedule wasn't going to fit. Also, I found out that trying to fit traveling to far away destinations within the maximum number of vacation days from my job was quite impossible. I came up with a sabbatical of four months in which I could travel and do my DM training in Indonesia. I told my manager my plan and had my Fuck You answer ready in case my manager said I couldn't do it. I was actually expecting the answer that it didn't fit the rules or that I had to have had X-number of years of employment first. I was expecting my manager to say that there was no space in the plan, that I couldn't be missed and that customers were counting on me, but that didn't happen.

What I learned was that if you have FYM at your disposal you are strong in every possible negotiation. I did not ask my manager for permission. Instead I told my manager what I was going to do, why and when.

A few months later I traveled through Sri Lanka, went diving around the Maldives, did my divemaster training in Sulawesi, Indonesia and enjoyed backpacking life in Thailand.

One insight I gained was that it pays to find out what kind of regulations and arrangements there are. I had withheld money from my gross salary every month for a couple of years and deposited it into a tax-free savings account. I didn't have to pay taxes on this money as long as it was in that account. I agreed with my employer that the amount in my savings account would be paid out spread over four months during my trip. I paid less tax on this because I went on unpaid leave and had no further income. With the money paid into my account during the months of 'unpaid' leave I was able to travel comfortably, pay for a week of live-aboard diving and even finance my entire divemaster training.

With renewed energy I went back to work. I did some fun and useful training and education that I had chosen for myself paid for by my employer. I worked hard again. I saved up overtime and got paid for it. I deposited it all into my FYM account.

A real Fuck You! moment and letter of resignation

A few years later I was held back from a well deserved, I thought, promotion. My manager had different ideas about my career than I did. I was instructed to do specific types of training that I did not like in order for me to develop in a direction that I did not want to go. I was supposed to meet sales targets while I thought I was doing great things for my customers.

I was told that a promotion wasn't going to happen, again, because of all the bureaucratic bullshit rules but that I would be financially compensated. This was a very clear signal. The universe was trying to make something clear to me. I couldn't ignore this. I waited until the bonus was transferred into my account and the day after, the last day of the month, I resigned. Without wasting too many words I told my manager that I was going to do all the things I hadn’t been allowed to do within the company.

14 months solo world tour

A month or two later I travelled over land and sea, across the Sahara, on 'public transport' to Dakar. It was the beginning of a 14-month solo trip through Africa and Asia in which I spent quite a bit of my FYM. It was the best destination for my hard-earned money.

During this trip I gained a number of insights:

- If you don't make any money, you don't pay taxes. I even got money back from the tax office during this trip.
- Someone was living in my rented house in Amsterdam so I didn't have to spend a single euro of my FYM on something that wasn't of use to me during that time.
- I was able to deregister from the Dutch health care system. I didn't use it for more than a year and I didn't have to pay any health care contribution. I took out a long-duration travel insurance for an amount of which I can only pay a few months of health care contribution in the Netherlands.
- I spent little during my travels. I had saved quite a bit and I had a reasonable budget but it doesn't cost that much if you organize things well. In the countries I visited, the cost of living is so low that I could do anything I wanted for less than €1000 (US$1200) a month on average. I spent my money on sometimes sleeping in a cheap cabin on a beach, sometimes relatively expensive wildlife safaris, almost always extremely cheap food and sometimes an expensive flight.
- From the budget I had set for myself I could travel longer than I thought.
- I had less and less need for stuff. I replaced some essentials a few times. I got rid of more and more stuff so my backpack was less heavy.
- I kept track of every expense I made, every single euro. This gave me a lot of insight. I started to convert money I did not spend into extra travel days. I was able to see exactly how many more days I could travel (extra) with my set budget because I paid (more) attention to certain expenses and kept an eye on my daily average.

Working for myself

The second part of my Fuck You Money I spent on starting to work for myself. The week after I got back to the Netherlands I registered at the Chamber of Commerce and started doing things that I enjoy, am good at, that other people appreciate and want to pay me for. As a starting entrepreneur I was not entitled to any benefits, while I had no turnover and no income, so my FYM was keeping me afloat.

It took me some time to get paid assignments and I certainly doubted my decision from time to time. Just before I hit the bottom of my FYM account things turned around. I was able to sell and soon I worked almost full time, earning more than when I was an employee. I put this money aside for harder times. I was no longer interested in owning an expensive car, laptop or phone as a consequence of my long travels and I now had to pay for it myself as a self-employed entrepreneur. I bought the things I needed for my work with a focus on functionality instead of looks, image or other bullshit reasons.

Life happens

I met the woman who would later become my wife and we enjoyed the good life as DINKY - Double Income No Kids (Yet) in Amsterdam, where she came to live with me. We bought the house that I had been renting since I was a student. We financed it with a mortgage based on her salary because my income and assets did not count according to the rules of the banks in the Netherlands due to my self-employment.

We were quite capable of not spending all that came in and we put it in a savings account. We didn't invest any money in the stock market because we didn't want to lose our FYM. We traveled low budget for a month (to the Andaman Islands) and I asked her to marry me on a deserted island that we had to swim for half an hour to get to.

We completely renovated the apartment and paid for it without an extra loan. We got married, my wife resigned and we went on a four month honeymoon to Japan, Vanuatu and New Caledonia.

Work pressure, stress increasing

We both worked pretty hard. Me with my own company. My wife in one corporate job after another. We lived well and didn't spend all our money. I had enough money left each month to keep topping up my FYM account. By now my wife had (also) got her motorcycle license and she bought her dream bike, a red Ducati. She did end up in work situations that didn't work out well. We had enough income enabling us to pay off extra on our mortgage.

Living abroad

We had said to each other that we wanted to leave the Netherlands and live and work somewhere else. I got an assignment in India and was negotiating with Australia for a job. My father became very ill. Our plans were shelved and I decided to spend a lot of my time with my dad during the last months of his life. I wasn't working at the time and I didn't need to. It was very important to me to be able to support my father. After his death we stayed in the Netherlands to be there for my mother.

During a vacation we decided to move to London because the large company where my wife worked moved its headquarters there. I got an assignment in London and within a month it was all organized.

London, more, faster, tougher, more expensive

London was fantastic and expensive, hectic and hard work but a lot of fun. We had rented a cool apartment in Camden with an extra bedroom and bathroom so friends and family could visit us, which happened a lot.

Investing in our real estate

We kept our apartment in Amsterdam and rented it out within a month to an expat family. In between we paid extra off of the mortgage and we invested in mortgage refinancing to lower the interest rate. Our monthly charges went down (significantly) and the rental income went up a few percent each year. Additionally the increase in value of the apartment is a bonus but does not directly increase our passive income.

We invested in an extension, we added 30 square meters for an extra living room and a new master bedroom. By doing this, our apartment became an even more attractive proposition for rental to expats. We paid for this out of our FYM pot, in cash, without a loan.

It's time for plan B: We are leaving

After a few years, and another semi burn-out for my wife, we discussed our state of affairs on the Mediterranean island of Formentera. How are we doing? How are we feeling about our life in London? How do we want to proceed? Do we want to stay in London and live this life? Barefoot on the beach at sunset and with a beer in hand we decide to pull the plug.

It turns out, once we think about it a little longer, that this is the moment for Plan B. Ever since I returned from my long journey and certainly since we got to know each other, Plan B is: 'Off we go, on a long journey, just the two of us'. Within four months everything had been arranged and we were on a plane, one-way to South America. With a FYM account of around €80K (US$95K) we will see where we will end up.

After a year and a half of travelling, we come back to the Netherlands for four weeks, mainly to see our family and friends, and we leave again. After another year of traveling we do this again and leave again. We learn to spend less and our traveling is getting cheaper. We visit cheaper countries and travel slower and our Burn-Rate, the average we spend every day, is getting lower and lower. More often we are in a country where our expenses are lower than the passive income we receive.

From Slow Travel to Nomadic FIRE

After 3.5 years of travelling we take stock again. We want to do things differently. We don't want to go back home but we want to travel less. We agree that we will look for a nice cheap place somewhere in the world where we can stay for a long time. We don't want to work and depending on the Cost Of Living of the countries where we live we can continue this lifestyle for a long time. My FYM account is not depleted. We decide to reserve $10K of this as an 'Emergency fund' to cover our first months of living if we want, or need, to return to the Netherlands. We also decide to change our lifestyle, wherever we end up, to make our Burn-Rate lower than our passive income. In short, we are FIRE.

We meet an entrepreneur on the Maldives and agree to help him to manage a guesthouse next season, on one of the beautiful islands where manta rays and whale sharks swim. We let him know that we don't expect any form of wages and agree that he will pay us a part of the profit, if there is any.

Locked Down in India

We return to India, which we find a wonderful country, and my wife joins a yoga teacher training course. Later we move to Goa and are increasingly confronted with Coronavirus/COVID-19. We decide to stay and move into an apartment with a kitchen and end up in the first lockdown.

We have lived the lives of retirees since then and we love it (I am 46 years old at the moment). We cook for ourselves and go out for dinner every now and then. We don't have a car, motorcycle or scooter. We walk a lot and we bought bicycles for longer distances. We spend very little money. Because our Burn-Rate is lower than our passive income, our FIRE account is growing slowly.

Why most people think about FYM too late

Why do most people think about what they do with their money too late in their lives? Why do most people always run out of money? Why is it so difficult to save? And, why do you earn more but also spend more, and more, money?

Partly it's a generational thing. I think the baby-boomer generation has had every reason to work hard all their lives for a comfortable retirement. This generation also likes to leave quite a lot of inheritance to their children and grandchildren. This generation hasn't given too much thought as to whether it's possible to stop working sooner, or whether you can take a few months, or years, off to do other things. Also, this generation has been able to make use of financial packages such as pension plans, partly funded by employers and government.

The children of the baby boomers are the so-called Generation X (1970-1985). Their life is dominated by self-development and self-realization. Generation X was the first generation to study on a widescale. And this is the generation that benefits from the wealth built up by the boomers, often held in illiquid real estate, which they will inherit.

Generation Y comes next, these are the millennials, and for this generation building wealth and buying and owning a house is less likely to be possible. For Gen X and Gen Y the future of pension provision is unclear. What is already clear however, is the shifting retirement age.

Generation Z is said to take control of life itself in shaping a happy future. These generations are given a lot of freedom and thus a lot of personal responsibility, which can also be experienced as a burden.

Designing your lifestyle with less bullshit and more FYM may well result in Financial Independence and FIRE. As far as I am concerned, thinking and talking about FYM and FIRE is more relevant than ever. Hopefully a larger part of today's working generations will take responsibility for themselves and become more financially independent of employers and government.

Why doesn't everyone do this?

I sometimes feel like the motorist who hears about a driver going in the wrong direction on the radio and says: "One going in the wrong direction? I see a hundred of them!" Clearly the driver, without realizing it, is the person going the wrong direction. In my life I sometimes feel I'm doing the opposite of the other drivers and wonder, "Why doesn't everyone do this?". It might well be the case that you are the one going in the wrong direction.

I think one of the reasons is because we are not raised that way. Not by our parents, not at school, not in society.

Another reason is, and I often come back to this in this book, because we care so much about what others do and think. We are group animals; we want to belong to a group and we like to conform to that group.

A third reason is because almost everyone suffers from lifestyle inflation. Most people start spending more if they earn more. We expect more and more from life every time our income rises. Something that was once 'desirable' as part of our lifestyle changes into 'necessary' as soon as we can afford more. We think we can't live without it anymore; we feel we have a right to it. Where we were once happy to be able to spend $1,500 a month, we quickly adjust our spending as soon as we have $2,000 to spend, and soon we can't imagine having ever made it with less than $2,000. When we double our income, we tend to double our spending as well.

Low-budget vacations seem a thing of the past, you certainly deserve more luxury and don't mind paying a little more for it. Changed requirements (your professional job) require you to buy a car. The promotion you got means you have to look more professional; the higher income goes to more expensive clothes and a more expensive car. The tendency to always buy the latest and the best you can afford is often largely due to the need to keep pace with the lifestyles of those around you.

Without stopping this and setting priorities, we will never have any money left by the end of the month, we never reach our savings goals, we never create enough FYM and we can never pay for our dreams.

Finally, the fear and uncertainty created by ignorance is probably a reason. We choose the safest option, the reliable brands. We believe what is said and claimed. We like to be fooled. We rely on market forces, growth, experts and consumerism. We keep looking for growth, more, bigger and better. We believe our lives can't be better unless we consume and buy as much expensive stuff as possible.

I hereby express the hope that after, or even during, reading this book you are convinced that things can be done differently, that it will become better for you by outsmarting others.

Why you can start now

There is no better time to start to create FYM than now (or at least as soon as possible). Don't delay doing what you can. Don't wait until you're retired or when you are less physically and mentally able, to do the things you once thought you wanted to do. Don't wait for a burn-out to make you re-think your lifestyle. Don't wait for an illness to force you to change tack or take it easy. Don't wait for your children or partner to pull the emergency brake and demand that you escape from your bullshit job. Don't wait until it's too late to escape from your lifestyle creep.

Starting is the most important thing. The first step is to make the decision. You don't have to do anything else yet, just ,ake the decision that you are going to save money for a goal to be determined in the future. You don't need to know how you are going to save money yet. You don't need to know what you want to save for yet. You don't need to know how much you want to save yet. Please just start saving.

The second step is to share your decision with other people. Again, you don't need to know what, how, how much and when. You can just share with your partner, parents, a good friend or reliable colleague that you have decided to start saving FYM. This step is guaranteed to have a huge positive effect on the success rate of whatever you want to achieve.

The problem with many people, and I often encounter this, is that there is a lot of doubt as to whether it is possible. I am convinced that it is exactly this doubt that is the most inhibiting reason. There is doubt as to whether you will earn enough money in the future, doubt as to whether you will have to cancel everything you like in your life now and doubt about pension schemes in the future. There is doubt about so many things in the future. And you can hardly influence all of these things in the future.

I realized a number of times while writing this book that breaking down the mental barriers is a much more important part than the financial barriers. The psychological, socio-cultural factors are much more difficult to change than the rational, financial factors.

I know from personal experience in my work with people and teams but also from my own life that you can directly influence your way of thinking. You can start thinking more clearly. I'll elaborate on that later when I share some insights from the book 'The Art of Thinking Clearly' by Rolf Dobelli. You can start thinking 'Smarter, Better, Cheaper'. That is looking for a win-win-win situation instead of thinking in 'trade-offs'. You don't have to see the quality of life decrease in the short term while you have no idea what you will gain in the long term. You can start to think more independently and try to care less of what others think and do. You can quit FOMO and draw up your own plan. You can start thinking 'tiny' and make steps smaller so that you can and dare to take them. I will discuss this later when I describe a number of ideas from the book 'Tiny Habits' by BJ Fogg. You can start dreaming and fantasizing about what is possible when you have saved FYM.

The only thing you shouldn't do is 'do nothing'. That's the only way to guarantee no success whatsoever. So, make your decision, please just start saving Fuck You Money.

The Latte Factor

The essence of the story about Zoey in the book 'The Latte Factor: Why you don't have to be rich to live rich' by David Bach applies to many people living in as many countries. "The problem of our personal finances," says the author, "is not how much money you make but our money habits and our attitude that we think we can't save because we never have anything left over." The book explains that there are three myths and that everyone has something the author calls the Latte Factor.

Myth 1: Make more money and you'll be rich.

"Most people think they have an income problem. They don't. They have an expenditure problem. If you make your income bigger you take the money problems you have and make them bigger. Your money problems stem from your money habits and they don't change because your income increases. The solution to your money problems is not more money but new habits".

Myth 2: You need money to make money grow.

"You don't need a large amount of money to build wealth. Start with ten euros, pounds or dollars a day, this makes all the difference. You don't need a big commitment to get started. What you do need is to face the reality of your situation and decide to do something about it".

Myth 3: Someone else will take care of you.

"No, they won't. If you pay yourself first and invest ten or twenty-five euros or dollars in your own future in any way then you take control of your life. A lot of people rent their home and have debts their whole lives. Pay yourself first and make it an automatic transfer so that you keep doing it, month after month, year in and year out and you're not dependent on anyone".

The Latte Factor is of course the expensive coffee you buy every day while you don't realize that it actually costs you a lot of money. What I find interesting is not the 'latte' but the idea that everyone has a few things where a lot of money disappears unnoticed or is spent on unimportant things.

The idea of the Latte Factor is that if you decide not to buy that one expensive coffee five days a week for a year and save the money at a 5% compound interest or return on investment, you will have saved more than $ 1300 after a year. Simply by not drinking that one coffee a day.

It's not about the coffee. The Latte Factor is a metaphor. It can be anything you spend extra money on which you could give up without too much trouble. The Latte Factor is not about becoming stingy, or never doing or buying anything nice again. It's about making clear what really matters, for you. It's about the little daily extravagances and frivolities, whatever they may be... the five, ten, twenty euros or dollars a day that you can just as easily save for your own future. It's about giving up something small to achieve something big.

You are richer than you think. It's just that you let the money run away as fast as you make it. Every month. A coffee on the go every day. Lunch out every day. Every day a can of energy drink or a bottle of mineral water. Extra television channels we don't watch. New clothes that fill our closets and that we hardly ever wear. It's not about punishing yourself or making sacrifices. It's about changing your daily habits.

Here's another calculation. Imagine you can save up to $ 25 a day by not buying that coffee and lunch and by making some small adjustments to your spending pattern, five days a week multiplied by fifty-two weeks, stashed into a savings or investment account with an annual interest rate or return on investment of 5 percent over forty years. You'll end up with over $ 800,000!

David Bach & John David Mann,
The Latte Factor - Why You Don't Have to Be Rich to Live Rich, (2019)

Reasons to want to be Financially Independent

With sufficient FYM you are independent of the income of a potentially useless job, an unpleasant work environment or an irritating and demanding boss. Imagine what it would be like to be able to say, "Fuck you!" the next time your boss puts pressure on you.

It's not about actually doing this, not literally. Rather, you want to prevent yourself from ending up in such a situation in your life. You achieve this because you have FYM and are financially independent or at least you think financially independently.

In the book 'Your Money or Your Life' Vicki Robin describes that Financial Independent Thinking (FI-thinking) is one of the keys to defining your roadmap for your new life or desired lifestyle. FI-thinking is the process of investigating basic assumptions that you have unconsciously adopted from people around you and noticing that there are frameworks that prevent you from seeing solutions. 'More Is Better' is no longer the way to happiness.

FI-thinking is about making your own map (I call this your lifestyle design). With this map you can choose your own path when it comes to your income and expenses. FI-thinking will lead to financial intelligence, financial integrity and financial independence.

Financial intelligence enables you to distance yourself from your assumptions and emotions about money and observe them objectively. Does money make you happy?

Financial integrity is achieved by knowing the true impact of your income and expenses, both on yourself and your immediate family and on the planet. It is knowing what is 'enough' money and when you have 'enough' material goods and what is too much, excess and clutter.

Financial independence is everything that frees you from your dependence on money to live your life.

Vicki Robin, Your Money or Your Life: 9 Steps to Transforming Your Relationship with Money and Achieving Financial Independence (2008)

I describe below a list of possible reasons why people strive to be Financially Independent (FI). Do you have another reason? Awesome!

FYM goals that give you more freedom and independence depending on your stage of life:

- Freedom to resign because you don't like your job and you want to spend time on something more fun. Because you don't want to keep a miserable job just because you need the money.
- Freedom to start your own business or work for yourself, which may not mean immediately making a lot of money.
- Freedom to make a down payment to secure the loan for your first home.
- Freedom to get more education because you want to, for which others do not see the added value.
- Freedom to pay for your children's education, without them ending up with a loan.
- Freedom to do work that brings in (considerably) less money but gives a lot of satisfaction or to do volunteer work that seems worthwhile to you but does not pay.
- Freedom to travel when, and as long as, you want.
- Freedom to temporarily not work for a long time to take care of someone, and to be there for that person because he/she is sick
- Freedom to temporarily work less to raise your child and to consciously experience the first years of your child's life.
- Freedom to take a family gap year and teach your children what the world really looks like and how it really works.
- Freedom to stop working and retire early, allowing you to do what you want for some of your better years.

Chapter 4
Why money brings happiness

Save now or live now?

Is it necessary to become a cheapskate? No. Do you have to be thinking about money all the time? No. Isn't it all getting a bit stingy, sober and restrictive? Of course not! Who wants to live off only the 'bare essentials'? Who wants to save money just for the sake of it being a goal and save for many years, never going to a movie, eating out or on vacation? Nobody, right?

It's all about balance. Life can still be fun. It is neither desirable nor feasible in the long run to sacrifice all the pleasures of life over a long period of time just so you can stop working one day. And then what kind of life would you lead when it comes to retirement?

As far as I'm concerned, it's all about living more consciously, making smarter choices and thereby improving your lifestyle and ultimately saving money. It's not about living a stingy, frugal life but it's about not spending money on things you don't care about. Most FIRE conscious people emphasize that they choose quality, durability, taste, value and fun but in a smarter way and not because neighbors, friends or colleagues have something.

Luck or regret

What is happiness? What in life is really important? Bronnie Ware has written touching and inspiring words about this during her work as a palliative nurse. She cared for and supervised dying patients in the last 12 weeks of their lives. She recorded their revelations in a blog called Inspiration and Chai, which attracted so much attention that she wrote down her observations in a book called The Top Five Regrets of the Dying.

Bronnie Ware writes about the clear vision people get at the end of their lives and how we can learn from their wisdom.

> *"When questioned about any regrets they may have had or something they'd do differently, common themes would come forward over and over again."*

Here are the top five regrets of the dying, as written by Bronnie Ware:

I wish I had had the courage to live a life that was true to myself, not the life that others expected of me.

"This was the most common regret of all. When people realize that their lives are almost over and look back on it, it's easy to see how many dreams didn't come true. Most people hadn't been able to realize half of their dreams and had to die knowing that it was because of choices they had or hadn't made".

I wish I hadn't worked so hard.

"This came from every male patient I cared for. They missed the childhood of their children and the company of their partner. Men I cared for deeply regretted that they had spent so much of their lives on the treadmill of a working life".

I wish I had had the courage to express my feelings.

"Many people suppressed their feelings in order to keep the peace with others. As a result, they settled for a mediocre existence and never became who they really could become".

I wish I had kept in touch with my friends.

"Many were so engrossed in their own lives that, over the years, they had let golden friendships pass them by. There was much deep regret that we had not given friendships the time and effort they deserved.

I wish I had made myself happier.

"Many only realized in the end that happiness is a choice. They were stuck in old patterns and habits. The so-called comfort of familiarity flowed into their emotions, as well as into their physical lives. Fearing for change, they pretended to be happy to others and to themselves, while deep inside they longed to laugh and have foolishness in their lives again".

Life is a choice. It is your life. Choose consciously, choose wisely, choose honestly. Choose happiness.

Bronnie Ware, Top Five Regrets of the Dying: A Life Transformed by the Dearly Departing (2019)

Blog by Bronnie Ware
bronnieware.com/blog/regrets-of-the-dying/

A Good Life

I believe, and argue, that choosing a lifestyle in which you make smart choices based on what you think matters goes well with financial independence thinking. Maybe the combination of these two ensures that you lead a good life, a valuable life.

Robert and Edward Skidelski summarize 'the good life' in seven elements:

1. Health
2. Security
3. Respect
4. Personality
5. Leisure
6. Friendship
7. Harmony with nature

People who consciously organize their lives can choose to work fewer hours in a week and gain a lower salary. Perhaps they can deal differently with their leisure time, watch less television and have time left over for active or creative affairs. There is social pressure in the perception of what is enough. According to Robert and Edward, 'enough' is what we need for a good life and not 'more, bigger, more expensive, better'.

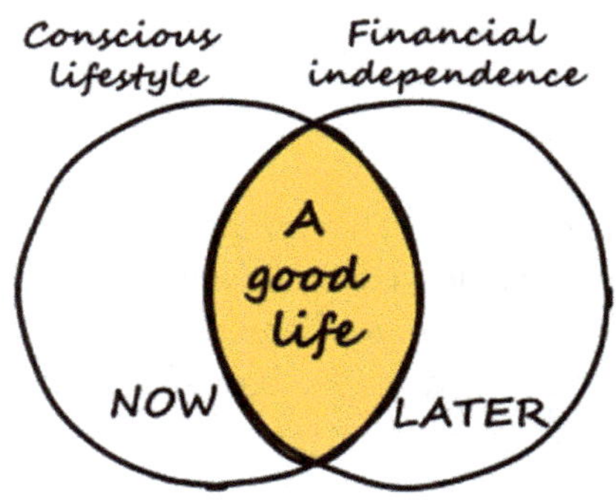

A good life, a valuable life, is a better life than a life in which you don't make your own choices. A good life is a life in which you know when 'good' is good enough and in which you are 'time-rich'.

When designing your conscious lifestyle, I ask you to take the above-mentioned aspects of 'the good life' into account. Consider how a 'Smarter, Better, Cheaper' lifestyle goes hand in hand with improving those aspects of your life that are important to you. I am aware that this cannot be done all at once and especially that implementing the changes and adapting your lifestyle takes time and effort. You should also take into account that you may encounter resistance within yourself, for example if you feel that you are sacrificing too much. In such a moment it is, I believe, especially important that you consider for a moment: 'Why do I want this again?' and 'What is the alternative?'

It's like deciding to use less sugar. You really want to get rid of your sugar addiction. You know that it will make you healthier, fitter or slimmer and you can avoid health problems in the future. Whilst you're not used to coffee without sugar it feels like a sacrifice. After getting used to sugarless coffee you will never want sugar in your coffee again. When your circle isn't used to your changes they might make weird remarks about it. Later they will respect you. All the while that you don't see a positive effect just think about the unhealthy alternative and you will immediately feel better.

My personal experience is that, now that I am a little older, I interpret the seven aspects of 'the good life' differently than I did 25 years ago. Personally I have to admit that there are a lot of things that do not fit into my current lifestyle that I used to find important but which I don't miss, and vice versa.

Robert and Edward Skidelski,
How Much is Enough? (2013)

Hedgehog model

A model that I have used a lot all my life is the 'hedgehog model'. The Greek poet Archilochus wrote: "The fox knows many things, but the hedgehog knows one big thing".

In Jim Collins' hedgehog model it is about finding the overlapping area in the three circles of "What am I passionate about?", "What can I be the best at?" and "What can I make money with?". It's about self-knowledge in these three areas translated into a simple concept that you can apply as a reference for your decisions. Even though Collins intended the model more for companies, I have always used it for myself and others, at the level of the individual.

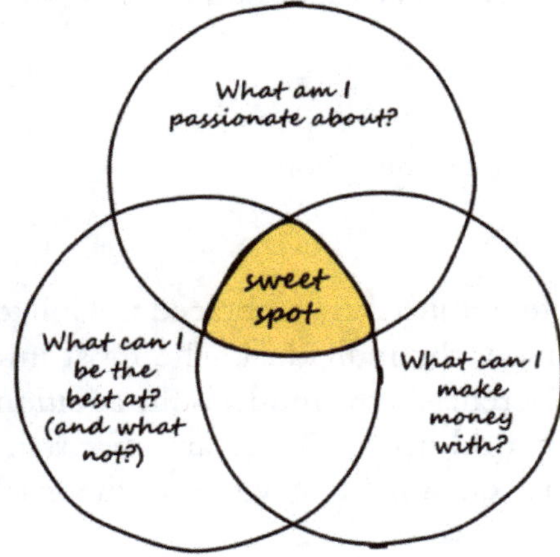

It's important that you do not see it as an objective or strategy. It is about an insight into the essence, your core and therefore the guideline for important choices.

I applied this model at times when I had to choose between education or switching to another department because I was no longer in my 'sweet spot'. Also, when I started working for myself, this model was my guideline. I think that if you apply this model to FYM and Financial Independence, it will help you to get a clear understanding of how to best organize your working life. It teaches you the discipline to say "No, thank you" or "Fuck You!" to possibilities that are not in your sweet spot and "Hell Yeah!" to everything that is in.

Take some time to ask yourself the following question:

What makes me passionate?

This is about understanding and discovering your passion. Where is your heart? What work do you do with the greatest enthusiasm? What inspires you inside, or outside, your company? Which core values do you identify with the most?

What am I the 'very best' at?

It is about understanding why you are good at what you do. What makes you perform better than others in certain areas? The emphasis and focus should be on your strength.

What can I make money with?

The important thing is that you consider what your economic engine is. How, or with what, do you generate profit, value or salary? What does a customer, client or your employer 'like' to pay you for?

As mentioned before, I started working as a self-employed person after about ten years of employment and I used my answers to the above questions to define the core of my business. I started to do only what I liked, what I had noticed I do well and what clients 'liked' to pay me for.

Jim Collins, Good to Great:
Why Some Companies Make the Leap...And Others Don't

Ikigai

I only came across the ikigai concept later in life but instantly embraced it. Unlike the 'hedgehog model' Ikigai is set up for the person, the individual. The most important difference in the model is the addition 'What the world needs'. These are important matters that do not bring you any financial benefit.

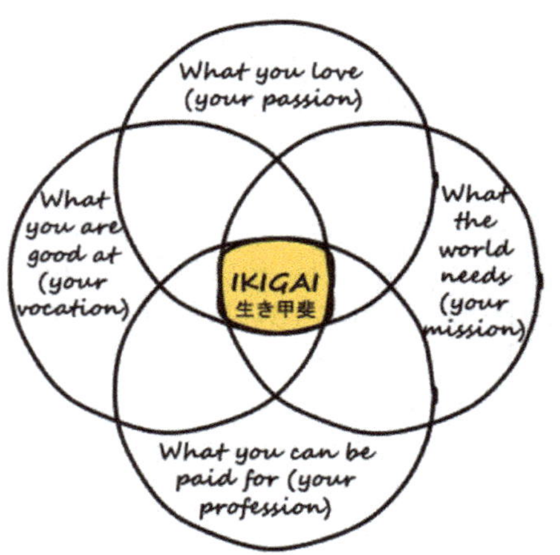

Ikigai has its origins on the Japanese island of Okinawa, which is home to one of the largest populations of centenarians in the world. Living by the principles of Ikigai is seen as one of the main causes for the high age of the inhabitants. Scientists describe the key to a long, happy and healthy life: healthy food, green tea, a simple active outdoor life, having a strong social network and having a purpose in your life, or ikigai.

The mysterious word ikigai roughly translates as 'the happiness of always being busy'. According to the Japanese, everyone has an ikigai, which a French philosopher calls a 'raison d'être'. Ikigai is also called 'your reason for jumping out of bed every morning'.

"Your ikigai is at the crossroads of what you are good at and what you like to do," says Hector Garcia, the co-author of 'Ikigai: The Japanese Secret to a Long and Happy Life'. He writes:

> *"Just as people have coveted objects and money since the beginning of time,*
> *other people have felt dissatisfied with the ruthless pursuit to money and fame,*
> *and instead they focused on something greater than their own material wealth.*
> *This has been described over the years with many different words and definitions,*
> *but it always comes back to the core of meaning in life."*

In their book, Hector Garcia and Francesc Miralles conclude with ten guidelines that they have distilled from the wisdom of the long-living inhabitants of Ogimi on Okinawa.

1. 'Stay active'.	Stay active and do not 'retire'. Even if you quit your official job, always stay active and help others.
2. 'Take it slow'.	Take it easy. Leave the rush behind and take a slower pace of life. Hurry is inversely proportional to the quality of life. As the old saying goes: "Walk slowly and you'll get far".
3. 'Don't fill your stomach.'	Less is more. Eat only until you're 80 percent full.
4. 'Surround yourself with good friends.'	Friends are the best medicine for confiding worries over a good chat, sharing stories that brighten your day, getting advice, having fun, dreaming . . . in other words, living.
5. 'Get in shape for your next birthday.'	Improve your condition with daily exercises.
6. 'Smile'.	Smile and recognize people around you.
7. 'Reconnect with nature'.	Reconnect with nature
8. 'Give thanks'.	Thank everyone and everything that brightens up our day and makes us feel alive.
9. 'Live in the moment.	Stop regretting the past and fearing the future. Today is all you have. Make the most of it. Make it worth remembering.
10. 'Follow your ikigai'.	If you do not yet know what your ikigai is, it is your mission to discover it.

Discovering your own ikigai brings you fulfillment and happiness and prolongs your life. Do you want to find your ikigai?

Ask yourself the following four questions:
- **What do I like?**
- **What am I good at?**
- **What can I be paid for?**
- **What does the world need?**

Within the framework of FIRE you can think of a situation what is your passion, you're good at it, the world needs it, but it doesn't pay? These are wonderful things to keep yourself busy with when you are financially independent!

What I find striking and interesting is the similarity between the ten 'wise rules' that are the secret of a 'Long and Happy Life' according to the inhabitants of Ogimi and the seven aspects of 'The Good Life' as described by Robert and Edward Skidelski. You could get the idea that you have to do something with this.

Hector Garcia and Francesc Miralles,
Ikigai: The Japanese Secret to a Long and Happy Life (2017)

'Good girls go to heaven,
bad girls go everywhere.'
Mae West

But who decides what is 'good' and what is 'bad'? For others perhaps incomprehensible choices and decisions aid you in what you want to achieve. What others think of your choices is irrelevant, because their opinion is usually based on incomprehension. Dare to be different, dare to break with routines or with something that is only done because it's always been like this. Dare to speak out, make it clear what you want.

"It starts with why," says Simon Sinek. It is about becoming aware of your necessity, ambition, wish, dream. This means finding out what your 'Why' is. Why do you feel that you want to do things smarter or differently in your life? Why do you think you will become happy if you do not have to work for a period of time or if you can stop working sooner? What makes you think you will be happy at all? You realize that money doesn't make you happy but that you want to have enough of it, so what is enough?

The most important question now is 'What do YOU want? I'm writing this on purpose with a lot of capital letters in the wrong place because I want you to pronounce every word with some emphasis and then one word a little more: What. Do. YOU. Want.

Simon Sinek (Video)
Start with why -- how great leaders inspire action

Simon Sinek (Book) Start with Why:
How Great Leaders Inspire Everyone to Take Action (2011)

Chapter 5
Why do you want to create FYM?

What are your dreams and ambitions? What do you want?

Will you quit your job and start what you're always talking about? Do you want to have more days of vacation? Do you want to spend more time with your children growing up? Why do you want to be FI? Let this be the motivating factor to make a plan and stick to it in difficult times. Once you have your Why you can determine your path towards it.

Several times me and my wife have thought and talked about what makes us happy. Even though we don't have the same hobbies and passions and we have different needs when it comes to, for example, comfort, we are able to think about a number of things that make us happy.

We have captured what we consider important for the first years of our Nomadic FIRE life, our dream, in a number of key words and phrases.
As you can see, this is not very concrete and that is fine (for us). It doesn't say in which country we want to live, how long and what we think we are going to do.
Still, this gives us a framework and makes it possible to talk about it.

Relax	We move slowly and seldomly; we find home bases everywhere.
Fun	We stay curious; we keep discovering cultures; we do what we like and we have fun.
Healthy	We focus on good, healthy nutrition and mental and physical fitness; we practice yoga/work-outs regularly; we enjoy but limit ourselves in the intake of alcohol, sugar and fat.
Peace of mind	We build routine and regularity into our lives, wherever we live.
Social	We live amongst and have contact with locals, local expats or other long stay travelers. We use modern technical means of communication to maintain contact with home, with purposeful attention and sufficient time for our parents and family.
Simple but comfortable	We sometimes enjoy luxury without letting it become our new necessity; we refrain from buying non-essential things.
Intentional	We choose this lifestyle; we choose to live an interesting, satisfying life with few limitations and little hassle; we choose to spend our time meaningfully without the pressure to make money.
Appreciating	We value local people and culture, including food/cooking.
Useful	We are open to do fun and meaningful things, we like to offer local help and would like to do house sitting, manage a guesthouse/resort or teach yoga classes or something similar. Potential income is nice but of minor importance and is not leading.

What's also not mentioned, is that we want to fit the above into our lives with the passive income we generate. We want to keep our Burn Rate, i.e. the money we 'burn', or spend, lower than our Withdrawal Rate, i.e. the amount we withdraw from our FIRE money.

What is also not explained here but is important, is that we choose a nomadic life, Nomadic FIRE. We have the desire and ambition to live in several beautiful places in the world.

Moonshot!

The first step in thinking about what you need for FYM and for FIRE is to think about your dream. Since Google has started to use the term Moonshot for projects like the self-steering car and Google Glass, it's a popular term used in the business world (but for me the word dream also works well).

More than 50 years ago, U.S. President John F. Kennedy captured the imagination of the world when he said:

> *"This nation must strive to achieve the goal, before the decade is over, of landing a man on the moon and bringing him safely back to Earth."*

As a result, the term moonshot entered our language as an abbreviation for a difficult or expensive task, the outcome of which is expected to have great significance. A moonshot looks far away, it inspires, it is feasible but also imaginative, it breaks with the past.

JFK's inspiring speech in which he expresses his ambition to go to the moon.

I would like to advise you to sketch or write down your dream or moonshot. Take your time for this. Find a nice place where you allow yourself to dream a little. Concentrate on what you really want, without taking into account all kinds of things that make it impossible now or in the future. It helps me enormously to capture this on a large sheet (A3 or 16") of paper, not too structured, it can be a sketch, a word cloud, a mind map, or a list of keywords. This can also be put in a document or mind map on your computer, preferably not on your smartphone because it's limited in creative space.

If you do want to do this on a smartphone, you can check if you like working in Workflowy (workflowy.com).

I then would like to advise you to daydream a little further about your future.

Capturing your present dream, your moonshot, your vision of your future.

This helps you and possibly your partner to be able to give direction, to come up with ideas, to come up with actions.

What do you want FYM for, what do you want to do with it, what is your reward for yourself? What will your life look like in an X number of years, when you have reached your FYM goal, what will you spend your FYM on?
Will you by then have reached your FIRE goal?
Why do you want Financial Independence, what do you want to do, what does your dream life look like from the moment you are FI or quit your job? What do you want most?

Continue on a new sheet of paper or page. Try to think as much as possible about the future and answer the following questions.

If everything is possible and there are no obstacles at all, what do you want to achieve?

Imagine that you can start all over again, with the knowledge and experience you now have. What would you prefer to do differently? In other words, what kind of advice do you give your younger self?

Imagine that you are five years on, and everything goes above expectation. What will your life look like in five years? What do you really do differently, what have you stopped doing, what have you started? What results have you achieved?

And how do you want to live your life in the meantime?

Building on the questions above, consider what your desired life and lifestyle will look like from now until then. Why do you want change in your current life, work and private?

(Why) do you want to make more conscious choices?

(Why) do you think you can be 'Smarter, Better, Cheaper'?

What does your desired lifestyle look like in the coming period until the moment of Financial Free Time or Financial Independence, i.e. the period of working, earning money, not spending it all and letting your money grow?

Use the points from the ikigai concept if that helps.

Find Inspiration

Find inspiration and think about what's possible, how others do it, what are good examples/best practices? Capture this and complete it on the sheets of paper or in your document.

Lateral thinking & generating ideas

Try to think laterally, by looking from a different perspective or from a different angle and generate your first ideas for your FYM and FIRE journey. We are all stuck in our own way of thinking, we live on routine. We think we have to make the same choices as our friends, neighbors, family. We have to break through this or at least let it go in order to come up with ideas. Think about what you want to say goodbye to, how you don't want to live anymore, how you want to declutter and consume less.

Write down ideas of what you want to start doing, think about what you want to stop, describe how you can do certain things differently, and think about what you want to keep.

Part 2

What

'I'm tough, I'm ambitious,
and I know exactly what I want.
If that makes me a bitch, okay.'

Madonna

Chapter 6
Designing your own life and lifestyle

Smarter, Better, Cheaper

Smarter choices, less stress, less nonsense, less stuff, an ultimately healthier and happier life. You'd think this is what we all want. I call it 'Smarter, Better, Cheaper'.

Smarter, Better, Cheaper is my answer to consumerism. In the book 'Stumbling on Happiness' Daniel Gilbert explores this as follows:

> *"Often what we think will make us happy does not make us happy. Are there simple optimizations that can have a dramatic impact on your ability to get closer to optimizing for happiness, instead of succumbing to internal or external pressure to stay on this treadmill of overconsumption?"*

It's about optimizing all aspects of your lifestyle for maximum pleasure or happiness with minimal expenses. It is about regaining control of your own life.

I believe that consumerism has taken full control of many people's lives and has caused too much irrational behavior. People work more, harder and longer, just to be able to buy more stuff, which in the end they can't enjoy at all.

The same happens to health, both mentally and physically, which is thoughtlessly neglected because so much is consumed.

Smarter, Better, Cheaper is about:

- Think unconventionally and out of the box, dare to look differently at challenges that can help you lead a good lifestyle that differs from others, instead of living from payday to payday.
- Know the rules of the game and play the game smarter. This doesn't have to be at the expense of others but you benefit from it yourself.
- Design your lifestyle, again a little smarter, make it easier on yourself.
- Don't care what others think or say of your lifestyle. Not everybody needs to understand you.
- Be patient and know that even small decisions can yield great results.

Through conscious and attentive living and making lifestyle choices based on the Smarter, Better, Cheaper concept you can strive for your personal combination of financial, physical and mental health. 'Smarter' is how you do it, 'better' is what you get, 'cheaper' is the result.

The fear that saving on quality means losing it is unfounded, I think. It is exactly the other way around. Almost every smart choice you come up with has a positive effect on your mental or physical fitness. Almost every smart choice will make you enjoy the things that are important more. Stopping with or cutting down on unhealthy food pushed by commerce is the most obvious example.

Walking more often instead of moving by car or public transport has a direct positive effect on body and mind. By mindful walking you see, hear, smell and experience more of your environment. With an hour of walking or cycling you burn calories and your brain comes to a rest. You could walk to do your shopping and even take walks to visit people and stop other expensive forms of exercise.

If you are more aware of what is really of value to you, you will enjoy a smaller selection of a better quality more than something you take for granted, or something you do automatically or because it is only convenient. Removing a lot of things that cost time, energy and money from your diary or shopping list will give you better habits and a better diet. And it's cheaper.

Daniel Gilbert,
Stumbling on Happiness (2007)

You can learn to think clearly

In the book 'The Art of Thinking Clearly' Rolf Dobelli describes in a fun way a list of 99 thinking errors or cases of irrationality he compiled. It's about not thinking clearly, or what experts call a 'cognitive error', a systematic deviation from logic. It is about deviating from optimal, rational, reasonable thinking and behavior. For example, it happens much more often that we overestimate our knowledge than that we underestimate it. Likewise, the danger of losing something stimulates us much more than the prospect of making a comparable profit. In the presence of other people, we tend to adapt our behavior to theirs, not the other way around.

Rolf Dobelli's wish is simple:

> *"If we can learn to recognize and prevent the greatest errors of thought, in our private lives or at work, we can experience a leap in prosperity. We don't need extra cunning, no new ideas, no unnecessary gadgets, no hectic hyperactivity, all we need is less irrationality."*

Examples of interesting thinking errors and advice on how to deal with them:

- Why You Should Visit Cemeteries
- If Fifty Million People Say Something Foolish, It Is Still Foolish
- Why You Should Forget the Past
- Why You Systematically Overestimate Your Knowledge and Abilities
- Less Is More

The book is fun to read and the stories are striking. I find many of his advices relevant and applicable to the desire to think differently and smarter, better cheaper than the crowd. Many of the 99 advices make it clear that you have to think more, think better and think clearly, and not waste too much time thinking about the past, what others think and say, not even about success stories. For every success story there are perhaps hundreds of examples of failures of people who have tried the same thing. The more choice there is, the harder it becomes to choose and make the wrong decisions.

We hold on to things we own too much, we attach far too much emotional value to them. We could better see all possession as something temporary and say goodbye to it when we don't need it. There is the risk of group thinking. Not speaking out if you are in doubt or have a different opinion may mean that everyone else is also in doubt or also has a different opinion but doesn't dare to say that either. In which case, you are all making a mistake. We are incredibly bad at seeing risks and estimating probability and we take far too many decisions on the basis of an expected return that may become reality in the future for only a few.

And why should you visit cemeteries? In daily life we only see stars and successes. Because success is made more visible than failure, you systematically overestimate your own chances of success. Behind every popular author you find hundreds of other writers whose books will never sell, hundreds who haven't found publishers, and hundreds whose unfinished manuscripts collect dust. You only see and hear from the successful authors and don't realize how unlikely success is. The same goes for actors, photographers, entrepreneurs, artists, athletes, architects, Nobel Prize winners, television presenters, models and don't forget influencers, bloggers and vloggers. This is called 'survivorship bias'. The media are not interested in the graves of the unsuccessful ones at the cemetery. Understand that you systematically overestimate your chances of success. Be warned and look for the unsuccessful ones by visiting the graves of once promising projects, investments and careers.

Rolf Dobelli,
The Art of Thinking Clearly (2013)

Choose your future, choose your lifestyle

In my opinion, too many people are too reactive in life, do not take matters into their own hands and have too little a handle on the direction of their own lives. I am of the opinion that you yourself must and can take responsibility for your life, especially for the decisions and choices that determine which direction it takes. I am of the opinion that many people allow themselves to be influenced too much by others who do not even play an important role in life. I think you have to decide for yourself whether you want to go along in the eternal cycle of fashionable trends that now and again determine that you have to wear jeans with flared legs, then skinny and then flared again. The only reason for this is that more and more new versions, new designs, new collections can be shoved down your throat.

Choose your future, choose life. It is up to you. Think about what you want your life to be like, design your own life, build it from parts that matter. Investigate what bullshit you can say goodbye to so that it doesn't take up any more energy, doesn't take up any more space, and doesn't cost any more money.

It is important to become more concrete, to 'life craft'. Tim Ferris calls it Lifestyle Design. I also believe that it's possible to design your lifestyle, determine your ambitions and make plans to achieve those ambitions. You can prevent life from happening to you or else at some point you'll be sitting on the couch and find out that your whole life has been one big lousy Sunday afternoon and wonder "What the fuck am I doing with my life ...?"

Just to be clear: I know that life cannot be planned and I know that chance plays an important role in becoming successful and achieving results. My point is that if you don't design and you don't make choices you have a much bigger chance of not succeeding. Most people then call that bad luck. If an opportunity presents itself, grab it, call it luck.

'Choose your future, choose life' comes from the music to the movie Trainspotting. The film has a bit of an intense way of explaining what can happen to your life if you don't choose anything at all.

Choose Life
Trainspotting - Movie clip (1996)

What matters to me is the message that life consists of making choices. My choices in life determine how my life goes. I choose to make the best of everything. I accept that from time to time this means that I don't quite live up to what society expects of me.

'The choices we make dictate the life we lead' comes from Shakespeare or Danny de Vito. Important here is the word 'dictates'. You make choices and make decisions and those choices or decisions determine the course of your life. You can't hide behind the lie that life happens to you or that it goes the way it does or that you hardly have any influence on the way your life goes. You determine how you react to events in your life.

The title of this paragraph ends with 'choose your own lifestyle'. What I want to say is that today, after reading this text, you can indicate a new direction in your thinking about what is important to you and what makes you happy. How can you organize your life with less bullshit and more Fuck You Money to simply create more freedom for yourself and become happier.

What is a lifestyle and how can you design your own lifestyle?

A lifestyle is a combination of tangible and intangible factors, particularly demographic variables and psychological aspects of an individual. These can include personal values, preferences and views, interests, opinions and behaviors. A lifestyle reflects an individual's attitude, way of life, values or worldview.

Nowadays, the cornerstone of lifestyle construction is consumption behavior. By buying certain brands, products or services that advocate a certain way of life, you create and individualize your lifestyle. Similarly, you also determine your lifestyle through the choices you make on how you organize your free time, which leisure and relaxing activities you fill your day with and which choices you make about your diet, food and drink, smoking and alcohol consumption,.

Lifestyle changes mean adapting things we have control over, such as changes in diet or daily routine. For example, choosing a healthy lifestyle means choosing healthy food, with more fruits and vegetables, spending more time on physical exercise and sports and ensuring healthy living conditions, such as clean air.

By consciously designing your lifestyle I mean that you take responsibility for yourself and the consequences of your choices. Not choosing is also a choice. If you don't dare or can't choose you can easily end up in an undesirable situation where, as mentioned before, you ask yourself "What the fuck am I doing with my life?" A choice is never 100% final. You can choose incorrectly but hopefully you will learn from this and you can always choose again.

With designing a conscious lifestyle I mean all the choices you make with the things you do and buy that influence on the one hand your Financial Independence and on the other hand increasing your independence from the (social) pressure from society in determining your direction in life. You do not automatically conform to the masses. You dare to and are able to make your own choices. You choose to optimize your happiness, whatever that is and whatever it consists of.

From a practical point of view, it's all about optimization choices like:

- Healthy, nutritious and tasty food, without paying for the image of the chef or the Instagramability of the dish on your plate.
- Become and stay physically fit by living an active life with sufficient physical exercise and relaxation, without paying for trendy drinks, magazines, unlimited fruit and soft towels at the gym.
- Get to work, on time and rested, without having to worry about gadgets like the new car of your colleagues or the pimped electric cargo bike of your neighbors.
- Have time for and pay attention to the people who are important to you, and don't have to talk about the number of followers on Instagram.
- Buy all the stuff you need but no more than that, with the features you demand. Do not concern yourself with whether it is the latest type or the right brand, has the latest features you don't use anyway or what you think your friends might think of it.
- Going on vacation to a place that suits you and not to a beach spot hyped by famous bloggers where you have to order overpriced drinks from the unkind haughty bar staff because it's so-hip-it-hurts.
- Have a pleasant and safe home, where you can relax, without worrying if your interior follows the latest trends or will ever be chosen to appear in a magazine.

Chapter 7
Four parts of your FYM and FIRE strategy

I distinguish four basic strategies Get, Keep, Grow and Achieve to come to an approach that everyone can follow, that everyone can get ideas from, that inspires everyone and that everyone can immediately start with. You will want to formulate strategies for all four components, with clear goals, plans and actions which you can eventually monitor, evaluate and adjust where necessary.

Get, Keep, Grow, Achieve

Get, Keep, Grow and Achieve are the activities you undertake to generate more income, to not spend all your money, to grow your wealth (save and invest) and to live a comfortable Financially Independent life or enjoy Financial Free Time without going broke. Get, Keep, Grow and Achieve are different parts. They are very clearly distinguishable but cannot be seen separately from each other. They can partly run parallel to each other but can also follow each other consecutively. You cannot perform Grow actions without Get and Keep. It is difficult to formulate Get, Keep and Grow goals and actions without having a fairly clear picture of Achieve.

Get

Work for your money. It starts with generating income. Your salary or the profit from your company comes in with some regularity and is enough to live on. How can you increase your income?

Keep

Don't spend it all. In other words, save. Actually, it doesn't really matter how much someone earns, at the end of the month it's usually all gone. I know a lot of people with good jobs and the same incomes but only few people structurally have anything left at the end of the month. If someone starts earning more, they almost automatically spend more money. People start living in bigger homes, buy a bigger car, go out to dinner more often, buy more expensive clothes, et cetera, et cetera.

Step one of your new self-chosen direction: become aware of your money behavior and create a conscious lifestyle where you do have money left over. How can you save money?

Grow

Let your money grow. With money you make money, it's that simple and that unfair. If you don't have money, it won't grow. If you are smart with your savings and invest it for your long-term goals, you will be surprised how fast you can make it grow and how much your FYM account or FIRE account will eventually contain. How can you grow your money?

Achieve

Making your money work for you. Whether you voluntarily temporarily have no income because you are volunteering for a year, or studying, or on a sabbatical, or two years of parental leave or never do paid work at all again. The FYM you have saved, your bucket list fund you have created or your FIRE account you have grown now pays for itself. With this money, the return on your investments or the passive income you can withdraw from your savings you finance your life. What does your life at Financial Independence look like?

Chapter 8
What is Fuck You Money

Whatever you want, and however you see the spending of your FYM in the future, it actually boils down to this: FYM is the money that gives you the freedom and ability to do something you really want or to walk away from something you really don't want while you are financially independent of the government or an employer. You can simply tell 'Fuck You' to anybody who wants to stop you from doing what you want.

FYM gives you the negotiating power in any relationship where the other thinks to have a say in your life. You can tell 'Fuck You' to an employer, a business proposition, coworkers, a client, a landlord, a government organization or a financial institution. With FYM you are in charge of what happens in your life.

Defining it in this way makes it more concrete, easier to organize and better to think about how much money you will need and when you will want to be able to use it.

Because you want to have time for other things in your life:

- Do volunteer work
- Start working for yourself or start your own business
- Pay the down payment for your first home
- To occupy yourself full-time with your passion, such as making music
- Take a year to write a book
- A part-time passion-job that doesn't cause stress but possibly also doesn't make a lot of money (like kitesurf instructor, divemaster, barista, ...).
- Doing an education, because you want to
- Going on a trip, as long as you want
- Temporary but long term not working and taking care of someone
- Raise your child and consciously experience him or her growing up
- Take a family sabbatical year and teach your children what the world really looks like and how it really works
- ... ?

Mini retirement - Mini FIRE

If there is no need to make money, it is much easier to choose to teach somewhere for a year, become a volunteer or work as a deckhand on a yacht that crosses the ocean. In the book 'The 4 Hour Workweek' Tim Ferriss introduces mini retirements as: "a series of meaningful respites throughout your life in which you take a break from your career, rather than taking one final retirement at the end". These are deliberate breaks, during your career and not only at the end, that you have because you are financially independent and you can afford to do it, with your FYM.

I think there are some differences between mini-retirements and the typical sabbaticals as I know them. I find that in practice a sabbatical:

- is usually (for a large part) paid by the employer,
- is more of a long vacation, not very 'conscious' or 'meaningful', not to 'reflect' well on your life, job, purpose, etcetera,
- is almost always with job retention,
- is almost always a one-time thing.

And that's absolutely fine, well done, do it! But when we talk about mini FIRE it's about independence. A mini retirement paid with FYM means that we have to take care of things ourselves, we want to give a meaningful meaning to this period and first of all we have to save enough money. I think that Mini FIRE or mini retirement is a great development.

Mini FIRE requires more preparation and planning and providing an opportunity at the end to get back to work or have enough money left over to ensure that you can find a new way to make money. It means making good use of all FIRE ideas and concepts, for periods of your working life, not just at the end.

Timothy Ferriss, The 4 Hour Workweek: Escape 9-5, Live Anywhere, and join the New Rich (2009)

I find Stefan Sagmeister's story very inspiring and a great example of how Mini FIRE can be done.

> Stefan Sagmeister runs a successful design studio in New York City. He works for seven years and then closes his studio for a year to explore new creative directions.
>
> According to Sagmeister, most people spend the first 25 years of their lives learning, followed by 40 years of work. If they are lucky, they enjoy 15 years of retirement.
>
> Sagmeister decided to cancel five years of retirement from the end of his life, take them in and spread them over his working life in the form of mini FIRE periods. He takes a year off every 7 years to experiment and discover new things in his life.
>
> It is wonderful to be away for a year for himself and he also gets more appetite and passion for his regular job. Besides this, the time off is very successful for his business, as he states that a lot of work comes out of it. All the new ideas he implemented during the next 7 years came out of his year.
>
> It turns out that it is not possible nor desirable for Stefan to do nothing at all during his mini FIRE. On the contrary, he undertakes enjoyable activities and the experiences he obtains during his mini FIRE periods, he describes as very 'fulfilling'. He gets fulfillment and feels deeply involved in what he does and gains a lot of inspiration; which he wouldn't get out of his paid work.

Stefan Sagmeister,
The power of time off

Also watch: Why you should think about financial independence and mini retirements, Lacey Filipich | TEDxUWA

How much Fuck You Money do I need

In answering this simple question you can lose yourself quite a bit. Calculating a correct target amount and determining a detailed target date is not necessarily useful because we cannot predict the future. It also isn't a necessity because you can already start not spending and start saving and investing money right away. A rough idea of what you think you need is useful and not very difficult.

Your Saving Rate (SR) is all the money you save in a period of time, for example a month, as a percentage of the total net income that month. Your average SR is an important metric and it can be a nice, inspiring ambition to increase your average SR.

Your Burn Rate (BR) is all the money you spend in a period of time, for example a month, as a percentage of the total net income or budget that month. You can also look at the absolute amount you spend, for example per day. It's good to keep track of these amounts for a while and see how individual daily totals effect your average spending per day and which individual spending on a day has the most impact on your daily totals.

You should also keep an eye on your Burn Rate while you spend your FYM, for example on a bucket list trip. If you divide your available total budget by the number of days you want to travel, study or go on parental leave you have your budget per day. If you keep track of how much money you spend each day and monitor your average Burn Rate, you'll be able to see in time if you're going to make it with your budget. Or if you have a budget but no end date you can extend the period by lowering your Burn Rate. If you have budgeted to spend $100 per day for 100 days and you actually spend an average of only $75 you can spend a total of 133 days with the same budget.

Your Burn Rate is also the amount you spend when you are FI and it is essential that your average BR doesn't exceed your Withdrawal Rate, otherwise you will consume the main component of your FIRE money faster and you won't be able to make it to the date you have set.

Fuck You Money for Financial Free Time.

You have come up with an idea of your dream, ambition or goal as discussed in the chapter 'Why do you want to create FYM? The second step you can take is to estimate how much money you think you will need. To do that, you need to decide how long your unpaid period will be and what you will do during this voluntarily unpaid period.

If you don't want to do paid work for a period of time but you do want to stay in your country, make an estimate of your total monthly cost of living without the costs you incur for your work (such as the cost of a car if you use it for commuting). Think about how much time you want to take in months. Multiply your monthly cost of living by the duration of your mini retirement. This is your FYM target amount.

Do you not want to do paid work for a period of time and live abroad, for example to do volunteer work or to be part of a totally different culture? Make an estimate of your total monthly cost of living based on the price level of the country you have in mind minus the cost of your home if you have found a solution like renting it out. Search the internet for Cost of Living Index or Cost of Living Comparison to get an idea of what your monthly costs will be. Note that such COL indices are based on an 'average person' and a 'normal life' in generally an 'urban environment' and adjust if you think your COL will be higher or lower.

If you want to live comfortably in the capital of a country it will cost more than if you go and live somewhere in the countryside for volunteer work. For example, if I look at a comparison between Amsterdam, the capital of the Netherlands and Pune, a large city in India, the comparison indicates that I need about US$1,380 a month in Pune to maintain the same standard of living as I can have in Amsterdam for US$5,900 a month (assuming a rented apartment in both cities). However, at the time of writing, I am in a village somewhere in South India, during the low season. A month's cost of living for me and my wife averages around US$885 a month, including renting a comfortable apartment.

I estimate that one year of comfortable living in a country like India, Colombia, Indonesia or Tanzania costs between US$1200 and a maximum of US$2400 per month for two people, so keeping US$30,000 as a budget sounds reasonable, and for many mini FIRE plans this is even on the generous side.

If you want to spend your FYM on travelling during your mini FIRE period, it is also quite easy to make a rough estimate. Calculate the budget for a bucket list trip using the following:

- Determine (roughly) where you want to go on your bucket list trip. If you don't know yet, this is purely to give you an idea of the costs so pick an example. Make an estimate of the travel costs to get there. The cost of a year-long return flight to anywhere in the world is unlikely to exceed US$1200 to US$2400. If you plan to make many intercontinental flights, estimate US$900 for each one-way trip per person.
- Determine roughly what you want to do there. Make an estimate of the average cost per day and estimate what special bucket list activities cost extra.
- Decide how long you want to spend on this trip.
- Calculate your bucket list target amount. This is travel costs + (average stay x number of days) + costs bucket list activities.
- Set your savings targets.
- Start saving.

My long trips in mainly not too expensive (low-COL) countries cost an average of US$95 per day for two people, including everything, even flights. Of course, you will have to figure out what it will cost for your specific situation and wishes. You can assume an average number of US$120 per day for two people travelling. This includes everything and is based on traveling in a modest way and not travelling too fast from spot to spot. Whether this is on the high side or on the low side depends on your travel style and need for luxury, the countries you want to go to and the number of complicated, long or expensive flights you think you will need. A year of this type of travel around the world costs about US$43,800 for two people, especially in countries with a low price level.

If you want to be able to go to more expensive destinations and have a budget of US$190 per day for two people and, for example, an extra US$1200 per month budgeted for things like skydiving in New Zealand and similar more costly activities, a six-month bucket list trip will cost you just under US$41,300. Almost the same amount, a different interpretation of the trip and half the time.

Keep in mind that travelling costs a lot less money if you take your time and if you arrange as much as possible yourself on the spot. We are talking about your mini

FIRE, so we can assume you have the time. You see more, you do more, you spend more time in one place and it costs a lot less.

I often give as an example a vacation or trip to Tanzania from Europe. In a vacation of 15 days, including travel days, you can visit Kilimanjaro, go on a safari in two famous wildlife parks and chill out a few days on Zanzibar island - all for US$6,000 per person. You can also travel independently, at a leisurely pace, throughout entire Tanzania, use public transport where available, arrange safaris to more wildlife parks, spend more days in the parks and hang out at Kilimanjaro longer. You can even go to the chimpanzees in Gombe park, which is far away from everything and spend two full weeks on the lovely island of Zanzibar – all for just US$6,000 with two people. Really! I speak from my own experience.

You can start saving right now. Say you want to have US$43,000 available for your plan and you want to take the plunge in six years. If you have 72 months (6 years) to save, you need to set aside US$600 each month to reach your goal. I deliberately do not take into account any interest or investment income. You put your savings away but prefer to keep them low-risk, which means you can expect little return. Can you save this amount of money? The most important thing is that you start saving. You can adjust your bucket list many times and your target amount and the timing as well.

Don't forget that you need to think about what you will be doing with your current home. Most people can rent out their property just fine to reduce the costs of keeping the house while they're away, some even make a profit on it. If you decide to sell your property or cancel the rent, you need to think about what you are doing with all your stuff and take these costs into account.

What you should also include in your calculation is any other income during your bucket list trip, such as some kind of sabbatical allowance by your employer.

Fuck You Money for a mortgage of a first home

For many people buying a home is the ultimate dream. However, buying a first home knows quite a few obstacles and these obstacles are getting higher and higher. This is mainly because you have to bring in your own capital and this is not something most starters on the housing market have enough of.

Many young people with a job and income with which they meet the income requirement for a mortgage would like to buy a home. They can often even reduce their monthly housing costs if the current rent is relatively high. However, if you don't have enough money of your own, you are more or less forced to keep renting expensively. This way you don't build up any assets. Because it is not likely that the rules and requirements will change positively, it is necessary to become more financially independent in this area as well. If you don't have any surplus value on a house and you don't expect a grant, all you have to do is take care of your own money. That too is Fuck You Money.

Once you have saved enough for this purpose, you can take out a mortgage, buy the house you want and perhaps even finance a renovation of your home yourself. If you immediately start creating this capital, you can assume that at some point you will succeed. If you don't start saving, you can be sure that you won't be able to build up equity.

Depending on the rules in your country, you can probably take out a mortgage up to 100% of the value of the property. However, there are additional costs associated with the purchase of the home, the so-called buyer's costs or closings costs. These are mainly application fees, transfer tax, notary fees, valuation costs and possibly advice and/or brokerage costs. Besides, you may want to replace the kitchen or bathroom. If you cannot borrow all this with the mortgage you will have to bring in your own money.

Check your country's specific values. For now, you can assume that you will need about 5% of the purchase price for the buyer's costs. A renovation can be as expensive as you want but for now you can set a budget of 5% of the purchase price of the property for a kitchen and another 5% of the purchase price for a bathroom and toilet. Later on, you can start budgeting more specifically. Now we just want to know how much you will need and how you can save this.

Example:

You want to be able to buy a starter home of € $250.000. The additional costs for the buyer and a possible desired renovation and thus the required buyer's own capital are a total of $37,500. This is your savings target. In how many years can you afford this? How much do you have to save?

You can calculate how much you need to save each month depending on the number of years you save. You can also estimate how many years you need to save based on your income and the part of your income you can start saving (the SR).

With a net disposable income of $2400 per month, you can calculate that with an SR of about 20% you need to save about six years to reach your savings target. If you can save more you take less time, if you can save less it will cost you more time.

Most people can increase the SR by, for example, handling money better or by making more money and not spending all the extra money.

Fuck You Money for the costs of studying children

Bringing up children costs money and most parents spend their money on what is needed for their children without hesitation. College going or studying children cost more money and many children will have to bear part of the costs themselves and borrow for this. On average, a student spends approximately $10,000–$12,000 per year on living expenses. The actual tuition fees depend heavily on which country you live in and what type of school your child attends.

Being more independent of the government and regulations in the future and being able to study without high student loans is only possible for children with rich parents, or for parents who see this as the perfect destination for their Fuck You Money. With enough Fuck You Money you can realize your children's wish to study and enter the labor market and the housing market without a huge debt. A mortgage is easier to get and more generous for a starting graduate without debt than for someone with a large debt.

Students are borrowing more and more often. Nearly 70% of Dutch students borrow money from the government and the average amount has now risen to €700 per month. The average student debt in the Netherlands has risen to almost €14,000 per student. A student who borrows €700 per month for four years must count on a debt of more than €33,000 without accrued interest. The current average outstanding student loan debt in the United States, including accrued interest and principal amount owed, is an estimated $32,731. The average debt among the cohort of borrowers who finished their courses in 2019 in the UK was £40,000.

The main disadvantages of graduating with such a loan are that the loan eventually has to be repaid, that interest on interest is accrued and has to be paid, and the restriction on taking out a new loan, for example the mortgage of a house for sale. With a large study debt, you will have to bring in more of your own money to get a sufficiently high mortgage or you will first have to pay off the study debt before you apply for the mortgage at all.

Example:

You have two children and have gotten used to the cost of living for your family at this stage of your life. You expect the costs to rise in the coming period and you realize that you have not been able to build up a huge amount of assets. In any case, you want to save at least $15,000 for both children to contribute to the possible costs of their studies and student life.

Depending on the age of your children, you will calculate the required savings amount per month. If you have 10 years left to save, you save around $100 per child per month and build up enough FYM in 10 years to have around $15,000 per child available at the start of their studies. If you think about creating such a study savings fund right at birth, you save the same amount in just around $50 per child per month. Again, by depositing as long as possible and as often as possible, you achieve the highest possible savings goal with a low amount.

Just do it!

I won't go into the actual planning and organizing of your FYM goal, bucket list trip or mini FIRE. I do want to give you an important tip: Make the decision to do it and make the decision now!

You don't need to know all the details, but you can make the decision that you are going to do it. Then stop thinking about the decision and only think about how you are going to realize whatever you want.

It is good to have made up your mind and it is nice to share your decision with others. Making and sharing your decision also has a psychological effect you create the feeling within yourself that you can't back down anymore, you're really going for it. Share your decision with others but know that you don't have to explain the reasons why to anyone. As long as you know why you want to save FYM or take a mini retirement, there is no need to justify your decision to anyone.

Making the decision and sharing with others also helps you plan things. You will see that it helps you to realize your dream. It helps you to start thinking about how you are going to do it and what you have to do to make it happen. By sharing your dream, you will make it possible for other people to help you realize this dream. In time you will be able to ignore the people who do not want to help you or the ones who obstruct you.

Chapter 9
What is FIRE: Financially Independent Retire Early

Background and history of the FIRE movement

The most important ideas behind the FIRE movement originate from the book 'Your Money or Your Life' from 1992, written by Vicki Robin and Joe Dominguez, and from the book 'Early Retirement Extreme' from 2010 by Jacob Lund Fisker. These books describe how you can combine a lifestyle of simple living with investment income to become financially independent and retire early, or FIRE.

Mr. Money Moustache's blog has awakened interest in FIRE among many people since 2011, especially in the US, and has helped popularize and grow the FIRE movement. Other influential books, blogs and podcasts continue to refine and promote the FIRE concept including Financial Freedom author Grant Sabatier. He works closely with Vicki Robin and popularized the idea of side-hustling. Deacon Hayes, author of 'You Can Retire Early! states that FIRE is about 'the freedom to choose to work or not'. It's less about retiring early but more about the freedom to pursue your dreams and ambitions.

There are big differences between the situation in the US and in countries like the Netherlands. The limited number of holidays in the US creates the urge for travel-loving Americans to travel for a long time. The sometimes very high salaries in combination with many tax provisions encourage tax-free saving for retirement. The differences between different types of people who FIRE in the US are big. Some are used to high standards of living and don't want to change that. Some make a lot of money, don't spend it all and save a lot. There are a lot of Americans living in high-COL areas making a lot of money who aim for retiring with a net worth of millions of dollars so they don't have to move out of their home or change their high standard of living and lifestyle. There are also many Americans who move to often low-COL countries for retirement, such as Costa Rica or Nicaragua. Recently Portugal has started to prove popular with this demographic as well.

In the Netherlands and other European countries many people have more leisure time during their working life than in the US. Due to historically excellent pension and early retirement schemes, it seems that people who want to stop working much earlier are frowned upon more. Now (2020) FIRE seems to rapidly be gaining momentum in European countries like Belgium, Germany, France, Spain, the United Kingdom and the Netherlands. On the one hand I think this is a reaction to a long period during which an entire generation X suffered from burnouts and work-related stress. On the other hand, generations Y and Z see that the government's safety net is wearing off, the retirement age is increasing and the responsibility for financial health more and more lies with the individual himself.

If you have to take care of yourself anyway and the retirement age is shifting to ever older, you can also become more aware of what is possible if you take care of yourself. It may be easier than you think to take time off and even retire earlier.

In general people in European countries don't aim to retire early with millions of euros saved. For most people a net worth of €500K - €1M is more than enough to live a more than comfortable life after FI, often in combination with a mortgage free home and some kind of pension.

Vicki Robin and Joe Dominguez, Your Money or Your Life: 9 Steps to Transforming Your Relationship with Money and Achieving Financial Independence (1992, 2008, 2018)

Jacob Lund Fisker, Early Retirement Extreme: A Philosophical and Practical Guide to Financial Independence (2010)

Mr Money Moustache
Blog (since 2011)

What, according to me, FIRE is really about

As far as I'm concerned there are two views, one focusing on the 'RE: Retire Early' aspect. The other view focuses more on 'FI: Financial Independence'.

It appears to me that a growing part of the FIRE community seems to be focusing less on the 'early retirement' aspect and more on the financial independence component. This shift in focus makes it less rigid as a concept, better applicable for more people and achievable more easily for most. I find FI, however you define it, positive, powerful and inspiring. FI still is an ambitious goal but in principle achievable for everyone who is prepared to implement small but important optimizations in life, just not spend all income and invest to make money grow.

Also, there are two views in the FIRE community when it comes to which extent you want to lead a sustainable life. Is it sustainable enough to consume less and for example ride your bicycle instead of a car because that saves money? Or should sustainability be more about the consequences for the environment and society? I think it's mainly about becoming aware of what you find important in life and how you want to fill in the aspects of a 'good life'. In doing so, you almost automatically become more aware of the importance of health, the environment, nature and changes in social relationships in society.

We can also distinguish two views where one focuses on saving as much as possible, the frugalists, and the other pays more attention to generating more passive income, the investors. Everyone draws their own plan. I very much believe in the combination of both parts and that in the meanwhile life can be fun, not too austere nor stingy but smarter. I think it is important that you choose the FIRE strategies that suit you and your situation.

You don't have to deny yourself everything in order to get as high a Saving Rate as possible, as high a FIRE target as possible or stop working as early as possible. I believe a balanced approach is needed and I believe ambitions are more achievable as a result.

Financial Independence does not mean that you have to quit your job. If you have enough FYM at your disposal, this gives you the upper hand when negotiating matters like your hours, vacation time, etcetera. You may want to keep working but only focus on what you really like about your job. With enough FYM you can negotiate to let go of the tasks that currently belong to your responsibility but that you don't like at all. Not only are you going to work less, leaving more time to yourself, but you are also going to improve the content of your job enormously. Smarter and better!

It's not about an escape from your career but about choosing a different, more conscious lifestyle. The best reason to retire early or work less is if you have a completely different vision for the life that you would like to pursue, but you cannot realize while working full-time. Most people who are Financially Independent and stop working don't stop working full-time at all, they are just going to do something completely different. They will do something they really like or find really useful and for which they don't need to be paid.

The foundations of FIRE

The fundamental economic idea behind FIRE is quite simple: spend less than you earn and invest what you have left at the lowest possible cost in, for example index funds, so that you become financially independent and you can fund your early retirement.

From a financial economic point of view there are a number of variables you can influence. You can earn more, spend less, grow your wealth and withdraw and spend your saved money at a certain rate for a certain period of time. You can think about optimizing these activities, I call this coming up with your Get, Keep, Grow and Achieve strategies.

Increasing the income side is not easy for everyone, but with a little creative thinking you might be able to come up with something that can lead to extra income or a passive income stream. Side-hustles, i.e. additional jobs or return on investment, such as renting out a home are part of achieving FI.

The expenditure side can be influenced by everyone. It seems easier to spend less money if you make a lot of money, consume a lot and live in luxury. Of course, it becomes more challenging if you are on a minimum salary and your expenses are already at a minimum level. But the message here is very simple: the less money you need to live on, the less money you need to save to finance FIRE.

Although these basic rules are simple, getting there is a different story. Achieving FIRE, just like achieving any other (financial) goal, boils down to behavior.

What types of FIRE?

Generally speaking, the following different types of FIRE are discussed:	And less general:
• FIRE • Lean FIRE • Barista FIRE • Coast FIRE • Fat FIRE	• Expat FIRE • Nomadic FIRE • Mini FIRE (mini retirement)

FIRE

FIRE, as I described it before. You spend less than you earn and invest what you have left so that you become financially independent and can stop working early.

Lean FIRE

With Lean FIRE you keep the spending on your lifestyle to a minimum. You only spend money when absolutely necessary and you save the rest. You can also extend Lean FIRE even after you have reached FI; as mentioned before, because you will spend less, you have to save less to reach your FIRE goal.

Barista FIRE

At Barista FIRE you strive for limited Financial Independence by using part-time jobs or freelance work to cover part of your expenses while relying on your savings for the rest. You use the 4% Withdrawal Rate rule, i.e. the proceeds of your savings and investments and you supplement this with a relatively low income that you earn with a fun and stress-free side job. Examples of the typical part-time jobs are barista, handyman, Uber driver, etc.

Coast FIRE

Coasting in life means making your life as easy as possible. With Coast FIRE this is a conscious choice. You consciously and consistently do the absolute minimum of what is needed and enjoy your financial independence and freedom by doing what you like and value.

This is someone who has saved and invested for FIRE and now has enough to cover a traditional retirement without any further contributions. Now all you have to do is earn enough to cover your current expenses. For example: if you earned $ 60,000 a year and saved 50% for FIRE or your pension, you now only need to earn $ 30,000 to cover your expenses until retirement or FIRE. You can choose to work less or opt for a job with little stress. Someone who is Coast FIRE has a conscious choice to continue his or her job or part of it as long as it is fun and interesting.

The difference between Barista FIRE and Coast FIRE is not very big and not always completely clear. The main difference in terms of FIRE methodology is that with Barista FIRE you take money out of your portfolio, at least 4% withdrawal rate and the portfolio doesn't grow anymore. You supplement this with income.

With Coast FIRE you don't touch your portfolio and you let it grow. Which means that you can work less because you only have to cover your expenses. You don't have to earn and save more money for your FIRE portfolio. As soon as the portfolio grows and covers your entire expenses you are fully FI.

Coast FIRE can be a good way for someone who doesn't want to stop working early at all. If you are sufficiently financially independent and don't want to stop working, you can start with 'not always working'. You can think about crafting your job in such a way that the bullshit part is removed and that only the fun things remain, the useful things, the things where you add value and the important contact moments with coworkers. Use Jim Collins' 'hedgehog model' here to determine which activities of your job are in the 'sweet spot' and which are not. What percentage of your time are you busy with BS things, stress, unfriendly colleagues or nagging? Tell your boss that you'll take a salary cut but that you'll now only occupy yourself with the things that matter. You will work less hours according to the same percentage. Your boss can spend the salary cut on hiring a younger colleague for whom it might be interesting to learn the tasks you've pushed off. You can offer to support and train that person. The salary discount you give yourself can either be paid out of lifestyle adjustments, you now have much more time to do things yourself, or else supplement from your FIRE account. And the salary discount starts from the top of your income, so depending on your salary and tax rate this means:

(net salary discount) < (gross salary discount).

If your boss doesn't agree, you can decide to start working for yourself and focus solely on selling and doing your sweet spot activities, possibly even for your old boss.

Fat FIRE

Fat FIRE means on the one hand not wanting to (have to) change your lifestyle and still being able to become financially independent. On the other hand, it means ending up with a fat account so that after reaching FI your lifestyle will also be characterized by luxury.

Fat FIRE is only possible if you have a generous income from work, business or investments. Fat FIRE is for the so-called 'High Net Worth few' in the world; people who have become financially very successful and who can quit work early, be it pop stars, soccer players, successful investors or the founders and then sellers of a successful company.

The idea of FIRE goes further than just stopping working and is more about conscious changes in your lifestyle and behavior. People who make a lot of money or are wealthy, and yet are interested in a conscious lifestyle and making smarter choices in life, can follow the normal FIRE strategy.

The most important and relevant questions and discussions amongst Fat FIRE people are about selling your company, managing a very large portfolio of investments, investments in companies or real estate, the philosophical question 'What is enough?' and of course tax optimization.

Expat FIRE

The world is easier to travel than ever before (pandemics aside) and there are many possibilities to live a comfortable life as an 'expatriate' after achieving Financial Independence.

I believe the main reasons for choosing this lifestyle are simple:

- Living somewhere where the weather is nice.
- Living somewhere where the Cost Of Living is (much) lower and you can live more comfortably for less money.
- Living somewhere from where you can easily and cheaply explore the region.

Nomadic FIRE

Nomadic FIRE is Expat FIRE without a permanent place of residence. The result is that you look at how long you can live in a country on a tourist visa, often 3 to 6 months and then plan a relocation. Another consequence is that you might make the place you rent a little bit less your home, you will buy less stuff, because you know that you will be moving on again in not too long.

There are as many forms of Nomadic FIRE as there are nomads, I think. We have met people who have bought a boat and sailed around the world. There are people who do more or less the same but with a camper van or a 4x4. There are people who look after houses or even resorts all over the world.

Living in a pleasant low-COL country in Europe for a certain period of time could be an excellent and viable alternative. At the moment, countries like Croatia and Bulgaria are popular among nomads looking for a place in Europe but also the south of Italy, Spain and Portugal offer good opportunities. An advantage of Europe for Europeans is that we don't have to worry about visas.

Tip:
Having a rough idea for the coming year or at least a shortlist for the coming years helps take away the restless feeling that you don't know where your next home will be.

Mini FIRE

I came up with this term in order to make it more in line with the FIRE theme, in general the term mini retirement is used. I elaborate on this earlier in 'Mini retirement - Mini FIRE'.

FIRE life abroad

The most important choice, after where you want to live, is whether you want to do this fulltime or not. There are a lot of people who live 'at home' for a small part of the year and in a 'nice weather-low cost' country for most of the year.

A second choice is whether you want to go for a leaner version or a fatter version. If you have enough FIRE money to pay the costs of living in an expensive country like the US or the Netherlands, you can also choose to live in a somewhat cheaper country. Here the budget you have will be enough to pay for a more comfortable and luxurious lifestyle. Or if you don't have enough FIRE money to pay for FIRE in your own country, you can choose to benefit from geo-arbitrage and still live FIRE in a low-COL country.

Because everything you do and everything you buy is cheaper, you can live differently. You can make more use of services that cost a lot of money in your own country. The hairdresser, beautician, dentist, driver, gardener and cleaner all cost a lot less than back home. The local groceries, vegetables, fish, and seasonal products such as fruit are not only much fresher and tastier, they also cost relatively little.

For the money you spend on renting a one-bedroom apartment in a middle-class neighborhood in the average city in the Netherlands, you can easily pay for a beautiful beach house in Thailand or Vietnam. For the price of simple food in an eatery in Amsterdam, you can have a three-course lunch with a glass of wine in the most picturesque villages in France, Spain, Italy or Portugal. From the cost of a cleaner for a day back home, you can hire a housekeeper/cook/caretaker for a month in the beautiful city of Medellin. For the price of a last-minute 4 day/3-night stay at a rather basic holiday home with 2 persons in California, we rent our modern and comfortable apartment in Goa, South India, for a whole month.

The main disadvantage of this lifestyle is that you are further away from family and friends. Depending on the distance and the possibility to visit home on a regular basis, it can also have positive effects. With the modern technical means of communication such as Skype, Zoom, FaceTime and WhatsApp videocall we now speak to our parents more often than before. In our old 'busy' lives there was always too little time to have a good chat and phone calls were often somewhat short and functional. Now we meet up around coffeetime or the appropriate time for a drink in the Netherlands time zone. Whatever time zone we're in, we spend some quality time together. This is valuable even though we miss the physical moments and we cannot embrace each other.

Another consequence of living abroad, depending on your chosen location and how difficult it is for people to get there, is that people come to you. The time you spend with family or friends visiting you can be the most valuable time ever. Our parents have visited us in different places around the world and the bond has become even stronger and more mature than when we only saw each other briefly during a family visit, dinner or birthday. Friends have visited us (every year) to spend their winter vacations with us. As an adult it does not happen often that we can spend so much time together. We have better conversations than when we only see each other once in a while during a drink or dinner.

At the time of writing this book we live in Goa, South India, just a five minute walk from the nearest beach. We go for a walk every day, wearing flip-flops / slippers and shorts. At the moment this is the place we choose. We live in a nice place, not between the tourists at the beach (because it's too expensive and not suitable). Important for us is a simple but comfortable living space and enough amenities to be able to live, sleep and cook. We get acquainted with local life and people. We do local shopping and prepare mainly local dishes. We buy seasonal fruits and vegetables. In the mango season we buy one pound of mangos for US$1; and they taste better than any mango for sale back home.

A topic that needs to be addressed is the residence permit or visa. Within your country or within a region like Europe this should not bother you but outside your country or region you can't stay for an unlimited period of time, you need a permit or visa. Because you don't have a job you don't need a work permit. This makes a huge difference and this makes things easier, but also arranging a long enough tourist or expat visa can be a challenge and in some countries even impossible. Some countries have a special expat-visa or even a retirement-visa. A retirement-visa has a number of important advantages but often you have to meet certain conditions. Usually you need to be able to prove a sufficient income for a retirement-visa. This can come from all possible sources of income, including investments. For many Low-COL countries the income limit is around $ 1000 per month. Sometimes there is a minimum age limit, usually 50 or 55 years old. Requirements for a popular expat retirement country like Thailand are: income US$ 2,000 per month or a deposit account of US$ 25,000 and you must be over 50 years old. There are also countries that make it extra attractive to invest, for example by building a house such as Costa Rica and Portugal.

There are many types of visas. Many countries are quite interested in bringing new citizens to their country, especially if they are not coming to take a job and are bringing in a steady stream of hard currency. If this is of interest to you, search online using the following terms: Passive Income Visa, Income Visa, Person of Independent Means Visa, Non-lucrative Visa, Elective Residency Visa, Rentista Visa.

One visa I have recently researched is the multi-year resident visa in Taiwan: the Taiwan Employment Gold Card. On the blog of a Nomadic FIRE couple, they explain that if you can prove that you have earned at least the equivalent of US$65,000 in the last three years, you are eligible for the Taiwan Gold Card. With these resident visas you can even work in Taiwan but you don't have to. The cost is less than US$300 and you get a residence permit, multiple entry and exit visa, open work permit, excellent health care, the ability to bring your partner or family and much more.

A Nomadic FIRE couple explains how to get a multi-year resident visa in Taiwan: the Taiwan Employment Gold Card.

A topic which raises a lot of uncertainty is whether you can move abroad to a more fun or idyllic place with growing up children and of school age. I do not deny that it is a big step and more needs to be arranged, but I also think that it can be great for both the children and the parents to live (for a period of time) in a different country. We regularly meet couples with children who go away for a year or more. They let their children temporarily go to school abroad or give homeschooling. There are so many things for children to learn (e.g. multiple languages) in other places in the world than in their home country. I think it's amazing to see how children (and their parents) learn about the world (social studies), cultures (history lesson) and nature (biology lesson) just by being somewhere else.

Within Europe there are also big differences in cost of living. There are many cheaper countries or regions where the weather is much better than in for example Germany, the UK or the Netherlands and where your children can still go to school. Mallorca or Portugal come to mind, where there is a large community of expats who do not work and still manage to live comfortably from a reasonably low budget.

Another topic of interest and for many people a point of worry or even the reason for not wanting to live abroad, is the fear of inadequate health care. The fact that as a full-time expat you are no longer registered in your country can also mean that you no longer fit into the healthcare system. Whether this is a good thing or a bad thing depends, amongst other things, on the healthcare system in your country and this is a personal decision. You should be aware that there is good private healthcare available for foreigners almost everywhere. I have been to the most modern hospitals in countries like Tanzania, Costa Rica, Indonesia and India, where all treatments are possible, at a fraction of the cost in the Netherlands and without a waiting list.

We have had long-term travel insurance for medical expenses and repatriation for four years now. There also exist expat insurances. We renew our insurance every year and in principle this insurance covers the costs of getting sick and being helped here and now. The travel insurance including medical costs, costs us around US$ 1200 per year for two persons, and is considerably cheaper than our personal healthcare contribution in the Netherlands.

We have claimed medical expenses a few times in recent years and this goes smoothly and quickly. I broke a tooth and had a crown placed. Firstly, the costs of this were just a fraction of what it would've cost in the Netherlands. Secondly, my travel insurance covered these costs while in the Netherlands I was never insured for dental care. The dentist was a well trained professional and the high-quality crown was made in a good lab.

Anyway, our costs for medical matters are very low. From time to time we have an issue and we go to the doctor or the hospital. In some countries it is free, in most of the countries where we travel it is very cheap. We once spent a whole day in a good modern hospital, had several tests done in a technologically advanced laboratory and even had a piece of coral removed from a foot in a fully equipped operating room by a surgeon. I was able to claim the full amount from the travel insurance, but it was only around US$ 185 including Operation Room, surgeon, multiple consultations, x-rays, prescriptions and medication!

I once had myself vetted once in hospital, a kind of health check. Running on a treadmill with all kinds of measuring equipment and having X-rays made of my heart and lungs, all very professional. Total costs: around US$ 65.

I am of the opinion that I do not want the choices in my life to be governed too much by fear and uncertainty and I accept my own responsibility for the consequences of the choices I make. I think that too often we are worried about things that do not happen in reality. I think we tend to be too dependent on others and institutions. To me, FIRE thinking is also about this kind of autonomy and independence.

Tip:
You can plan a (somewhat longer) trip well before FI and instead of being on vacation, you can live somewhere temporarily to try out Expat FIRE life. For this scenario, you need to be looking for a different kind of place, a different kind of accommodation and a different way of spending your time than when you are a tourist. You will experience what it is like to do your local shopping and organize yourself, just start with a local SIM card. You can see how you experience it and how it goes, which helps later to decide if you really want to take the bigger step and if the place you have in mind is the right one.
Make sure you have sufficient available travel funds. The Cost of Living may be low but you should consider a few potentially expensive flights, for fun or in case of an emergency. Last minute travel needs are the most expensive and having FYM in an emergency fund takes the stress out of buying expensive last-minute tickets when really needed.
Plan your vacation to be with family or friends well in advance. Whether people come to visit you during their vacation, or you go to them for a vacation, the distance makes it more difficult to be in the same place at the same time.

How much money do I need to FIRE?

Short answer: You are FIRE when your living expenses are lower than the proceeds of your assets for the entire period that you do not want to work.

The feasibility of your FIRE plan largely depends on determining your FIRE strategy, your choice of a form such as Lean, Barista, Fat, Expat FIRE and ultimately on the choices and events in your life.

For Lean, Barista and Expat FIRE your expenses can be lower if you are FI than for regular FIRE or Fat FIRE. You simply need less money and that can mean that you are FI sooner, can stop working sooner, can start the rest of your (FIRE) life sooner or that you get more value for money, you can do more from your FIRE.

The hardest to predict and calculate are the costs of your life. If FI is still far away for you it is difficult to estimate the financial impact of your life, whether or not you have a partner, whether or not you both have a paid job, whether or not you raise a child or several children.

Before you can actually start calculating, you need to consider a number of things. What do you want your lifestyle to look like when you stop working and what are the appropriate total costs?

Do you have a FIRE target date, a date on which you want to be FI? You can set your target amount and target date and use them as input to figure out how much you need to save. If you do not have a target date but you do have your savings potential and your target amount, you can use this as input and calculate your potential FIRE date.

Would you like to build up a FIRE fund only for the years you want to stop working earlier or also for the period from your retirement age as a supplement to a possible pension? Can you expect income or social security during retirement?

Do you want to keep your assets or wealth until the end? In other words, can you draw up your FIRE fund and use all your money or do you want to keep the main part of your capital to make a passive income from it until your death and leave your wealth behind when you die?

Do you expect to receive, with high probability, certain amounts of money such as inheritances, policies or annuities?

The 4% rule to calculate your FIRE number

The most commonly given short answer to the question 'How much money do I need for FIRE?' in the FIRE community is simple and concrete: 25 times your expected annual expenditure. This is based on the, for some people holy, 4% rule. I want to emphasize right away that this is only a rule of thumb. Also, recently there have been talks about calling it the 5% rule. There are many different opinions about the use of the 4% rule of thumb. The only thing everyone agrees on is that it is easy to use.

Numerous studies have been done. The researchers looked at the development of all shares and bonds over a period of 15 to 30 years. If you include all the movements, dips and crashes, you will see that in some cases you end up with a much higher amount and in some cases, you end up with a much lower amount. If you calculate with 4% withdrawals from your portfolio, it is most likely that you will not run out of money in the 30-year period. That is why we speak of a Safe Withdrawal Rate (SWR). In many cases, especially if you invest in, for example, well spread indextrackers (ETFs), the portfolio will grow faster than 4% and grow faster than your Withdrawal Rate of 4%.

On www.firecalc.com/ you can read about the research and methods. You can fill in your own details to see how your portfolio would have developed through history, taking into account annual withdrawals and fees.

You can also make the following calculation. If you take into account an average return of 4% and you want to make a monthly withdrawal of US$ 1,000 without your principal shrinking, you have to earn 12 (months) x US$ 1,000 = US$ 12,000 return per year on your capital. Because your return is US$ 12,000 = 4% you can say that 100% = US$ 300,000.

In other words, with a capital of US$ 300,000 at a yield of 4% (which is 12,000 per year) you can withdraw US$ 12,000 per year and your principal will remain US$ 300,000, to infinity.

Divide US$300,000 by US$12,000 = 25 as well as divide 100% by 4% = 25. Hence you can say that the 4% rule translates into 25 times your annual spending.

The 4% SWR rule of thumb is based on simulations with historical figures and therefore gives no guarantee for the future. There is a chance that the market will crash and that will be particularly bad for the people who are at that moment approaching FI. It is your money. You do what you want with it. If everything goes well and you have a higher return and more money, you can withdraw more. If the market collapses and you want to maintain your portfolio, cut your spending a bit and see how it develops.

The percentage of 4% is probably far too conservative for most people earning wages and building up a pension. The result of the low 4% or high 25 X-factor is a considerably high FIRE target number. Probably you will have to try very hard to get a high enough SR to get close to this goal. It probably seems that you don't have enough time to save this amount. The high target amount can be a deterrent. Don't be put off. Start saving and investing and recalibrate in the meantime. If you don't recalibrate the target amount, you will probably end up with too much capital at the time of FI. This means you could have saved less or even stopped working sooner.

The 4% rule is a reasonable rule of thumb if your goal is still a long way off and if it encourages you to take action, i.e. start saving and investing. The further away you look, the more uncertain the future becomes. If you are still a long way from FI, it is especially difficult to estimate what is going to happen in your life that will have an impact on your finances, both on the income and expenditure side. There is not much to plan yet. However, you can already start FI thinking and saving, as I have indicated in several places in this book. You can then see where you stand from time to time and make adjustments where necessary. Depending on life events and lifestyle developments, your wishes and goals will change. Only when you get closer to FI it becomes more meaningful to actually plan.

Determining how much you actually think you need

Determining how much you think you really need depends very much on your life course and the events that cost you money or not, and on the lifestyle you want to have when you stop working.

The average Dutch person who is currently retired receives a certain percentage of the last-earned salary as a pension. The average pension varies enormously but is currently around €2845 net per month (€35,000 per year). This amount is the sum of all sources of income (e.g. state pension, employee pension and any savings accounts or annuities). What do you think is a real 'income' needed for you when you stop working?

The average Dutch person who is currently retired, lives in a fairly large house and owns on average one and half middle-class car, even after the children have left the house and have become independent a long time ago. The expenses of the average early retired person go down considerably after a few years of nice vacations and long trips. If you are already engaged in a conscious lifestyle how much do you think you will need when you stop working? What would you like to be able to do? Where do you want to live? What do you think you will really need by then? That is the amount of money you need to calculate.

The now retired generation, the baby boomers, is the richest generation ever and it is also the generation that will die the richest. Many baby boomers have worked all their lives, often their mortgages have long been repaid and they have a good pension. Often they benefited from the best years on the stock market and they use up most of their assets before they die because the capital in their home is illiquid. How do you see this for yourself? How important is it to you that you leave money behind? When calculating how much you need for FIRE can you already take into account that you will draw from your FIRE capital?

You can make a personal analysis. You can work out one or more scenarios in a spreadsheet in which you take into account your specific situation and issues such as pension, possible inheritances or annuities/purchases and pulling your money out of illiquid assets like your house. Also, you can take into account expenses that limit your disposable income for a long period of time and thus reduce your SR like the costs of raising children. It is also up to you to decide whether or not to keep your assets until the end.

Even in the most specific models and scenarios you will have to realize that it is a simplification of reality. Predictions based on averages over a long period of time might be somewhat guiding but still nothing more than that. The only thing you can be sure of is that there will be changes and that investment results can also sometimes disappoint.

You'll never know what kind of return you're going to make in the future. That makes planning for the future extremely difficult. You can define your wishes and dreams and use them to determine your Get, Keep and Grow strategy, devise your savings plan, determine your investment strategy and choose the asset allocation that fits your profile and goals. But you can't do much more than that. Only a few years before you reach your goal does it make sense to plan.

What is advised anyway is to keep your actual Withdrawal Rate (during the period of withdrawal of money) flexible. It is better to withdraw less (lower WR) in times of reduced portfolio performance and safely withdraw more (higher WR) during a recovery period. In practice this will not be achievable for everyone but one of the best strategies to survive longer with your investments is to just spend less when the market is struggling or to find a job for extra income.

Whether or not to take into account an expected inheritance

The current generation of pensioners, the baby boomers, are sitting on a large pot of money and mostly fully paid off houses. The current generation of workers, generation X and millennials, will probably inherit more than ever. I think that if you expect to inherit a considerable amount of money somewhere in the next thirty years you can take this into account when calculating your FIRE number and how much you will have to save in the coming years.

The inheritance or financial support simply means that you will reach the FIRE target number sooner. Keep in mind that humans really are getting older and older and the Baby Boomers generation can statistically count on turning eighty or ninety. We should also take into account that today's young elderly people, now between 50 and 65 years of age, find it more important to continue their current lifestyle after retirement and might not want to leave their children a large inheritance.

4% rule and draw from your capital to depletion

I may have a slightly different opinion about the endgame. I want my capital to approach 'zero' at the moment that I, or my partner depending on who goes last, dies. This is a bit of a 'hard' statement and it does not have to be exactly zero; there may certainly be some left over for my nieces (we do not have and will not have children). I think it's a shame to die rich and not to use my hard-earned and saved FIRE money during my life. But I don't want to run out too soon and have no home or have no FYM left for the last years of my life.

You can formulate your withdrawal strategy from FI onwards. Again, do not lose yourself in the details and uncertainties but if you want to know what your FIRE goal is you need to have a withdrawal strategy as well. In fact, if you do not take into account withdrawing at the expense of your principal, then your FIRE goal will be higher and you need to save more. The most difficult part of this calculation is that you don't know when you will die but you can make assumptions and, for example, assume a scenario in which you want to provide yourself with income for 20 years because you want to retire 20 years earlier than the official retirement age in your country and then you want to provide yourself with additional income on top of the expected pension for another 20 years. If you want to give yourself US$ 3,000 a month for the first 20 years and US$ 1,500 a month for the second 20 years, it will cost you about one million dollars in payments. How high does your FIRE fund have to be to cough that up?

Most of the articles talk only about a withdrawal rate of 4%. This means if you manage to save US$ 900.000 for FIRE you can pay yourself US$ 3,000 every month without the principal decreasing, at 4% interest. If your capital yields 4%, you'll be left with the US$ 900K at the end and I think that's a shame.

How much money do you need if you want to end up around zero? You have to test this calculation for your own situation but I come at US$ 718,000. If you have a FIRE fund of US$ 718,000 you can pay yourself US$ 3,000 every month for 40 years and then it is finished at the end. I take into account 4% interest. What is extremely important to note here is that it is impossible to estimate whether you will achieve a certain return and whether you run the risk that your portfolio has actually dropped in value enormously at the moment you want to withdraw.

What does this mean and why is it important? You have to save the difference between a FIRE goal of US$ 900K and US$ 700K in the time remaining. If you have 20 years to do so you have to save about US$500 extra per month for the 'die-rich' scenario than for the 'die-poor' scenario.

Sample calculations
FIRE target: withdraw capital or not

When can I stop working?

If you know how much money you need (your FIRE number) and you know how much money you can save each month from your net disposable income (your saving potential), you can calculate how many years you have to work and save this amount to actually stop working. In the worksheet 'When to stop working' I give some example calculations. You can vary the data. The calculations below use the 4% rule of thumb. In a later section I discuss how you can calculate in a different way and how you can come to a more realistic and feasible estimate using scenarios.

Fill in your net disposable income	$5,000
Enter your target savings amount per month	$2,000
Saving Rate	40%
You save per year	$24,000
Your FIRE target amount	$900,000
In how many months can you stop working	254
That means in a number of years:	21

If you want to estimate how much you need to save each month in order to be able to stop working after a desired number of years, you can also calculate that.

With a monthly family income of $5,000, an expected return of 5% and an SR of 10% you save $500 monthly and spend $ 4,500 to live. Your FIRE target is $1,350,000. You can stop working after 50.2 years.

With the same income and a SR of 20% you save $ 1,000 monthly and use $4,000 to live on. Your FIRE goal is $1,200,000 and you can stop working after 35.9 years. With a SR of 40% you save $2,000 monthly and use $3,000 to live. Your FIRE goal is $900,000 and you can stop working after 21.2 years.

If you want to know how much you have to save for a certain period of not working, from FI to retirement age for example, you can also calculate that.

I am now 35 years old. I want to stop working in 15 years, at the age of 50. I want to finance the period from early retirement to retirement at the age of 67. From FI to pension are 17 years. I want to spend $2,000 a month from early retirement to retirement. My FIRE target is $408,000. With the income $5,000 and expected return 5% I will have to save $1,526 per month for 17 years or an SR% 31%.

Example calculations
'When to stop working'

For the diehards an attempt to come to a realistic and correct estimate.

I have explained the easiest and most used way to calculate your FIRE number. If you are still a long way from FI at the moment this is a good way to calculate it. However, a number of factors are not taken into account when calculating with the 4% or 25X rule of thumb. There is no perfect way to do this, the future is too uncertain, there are simply too many variables that are constantly changing. Again, I advise you not to lose yourself in the details.

Start saving money, increase your SR by spending less, grow your investments. While you've set all this in motion, you can later look at the numbers you've calculated. You will adjust them based on changing circumstances and you may use different calculation methods based on new insights.

A reason to apply a 'better' calculation method to your FIRE number may be that the FIRE number you calculated seems unreasonably high and therefore unfeasible. Read the following and see if you can estimate your FIRE number better.

Making a realistic estimate

The most accurate way to calculate how much money you need to become FI (your FIRE target amount) is to make a realistic estimate of your total expenses and income during the entire FIRE period. For example, you can assume that once the mortgage of your house has been paid off you will no longer have any mortgage costs. You can also take into account an inheritance, the surplus value of your home and the fact that you are building up a pension and therefore only have to bridge a relatively short period of time.

The most accurate way to calculate how long you need to save your FIRE target amount is to assume and take into account your current wealth situation, inflation, the possibility to save more (SR increase) through salary increases, and the restricting effect of life events for you to save money during the years of wealth accumulation.

You can, for example, make an estimate of the costs of a bringing up child and the effect on your SR.

Net Worth

Your wealth, or your Net Worth, is made up of a number of components and depending on your situation they do not or not fully count towards your FI net worth. Assets from which you cannot get a return to pay for expenses do not count as long as you cannot use them for this purpose. Probably the most important illiquid part of your assets is your home.

An example of how to calculate Net Worth (dummy data):

Net Worth	Today
Pay	
Current account	$1
Current account partner	$2
Current account joint account	$3
Save	
Private savings account - Bank	$4
Private savings account partner - Bank	$5
Private joint account savings account - Bank	$6
Pension saving	
Pension saving account (not withdrawable) - Bank	$7
Invest	
Shares - Investment Account	$5
Index funds - Investment account	$10
Home	
Property current market value	$30
Mortgage current outstanding	$(20)
Mortgage savings current balance	$10
Total assets (Net Worth) (total sum)	$63
FIRE assets (excluding house and pension)	$36
FIRE assets after sale house (excluding pension)	$56
Not withdrawable until retirement	$7

As long as you live in your house (which may have been fully paid off at your FI moment) you benefit from lower monthly costs because you do not have to pay any mortgage charges (interest and amortization) - you live for free. But these assets are illiquid meaning they do not generate an income that you can use to pay for your expenses and you cannot convert it to a liquid type of asset because you live in the house yourself. It therefore does not count towards your FI capital. This also applies to other assets like a car.

You can already imagine that at some point you want to liquidate this capital. You can take out a reverse mortgage to supplement your pension. You can sell your house and downsize, part of your assets will then become liquid. You can rent out your house and start living elsewhere yourself, you will immediately generate passive income with which you will be able to cover expenses. However, if you need to rent a house elsewhere to live your living costs will increase compared to living in a fully paid off house.

Expenses

You are FI if your expenses are less than your return on assets and other passive income. When correctly estimating your total expenses at the time of FI you have to take a number of factors into account. If you make this estimation on the basis of your current spending you will have to keep an eye on how your spending develops in the future. If necessary adjust your estimation and therefore your FI goals - do this once a year.

I describe here a calculation example with a current disposable income of $,3000 per month of which 50% is currently spent on essential needs, 30% on personal expenses and 20% is saved.

If you will have your own house fully paid off at the time of FI you no longer pay for the mortgage. Because you have reached your FI goal ou don't have to save anymore. The amount you need from FI is lower.

	Now	FI required
Net disposable	$3,000	$1,400
Spend on:		
Mortgage	$1,000	
House other expenses	$250	$250
Other	$250	$250
Personal expenses	$900	$900
Save	$600	

If you make an estimate based on your current disposable income and expenses and take the above into account, you will see that what you would need to pay for your expenses is less than half of your current disposable income.

You can now calculate your FIRE amount or FI number and how long it will take you to save it with a savings amount of $600 per month (see the worksheet for calculations):

FI target based on FI expenses (25x rule)	$1,400	$420,000
Expected return on investments		5%
Number of years until FI target is reached		27

Revenues

Your salary will probably increase during the period in which you build up your FIRE capital. You can be sensible and use a large part of your salary increase to save for FYM and FIRE. Your Saving Rate will increase as a result. For simplicity of this example, I assume that it is a net salary increase on top of inflation.

	Now	After 27 yrs
Salary - increases by 2.5% on average:	$3,000	$5,843
Saving - goes from 20% to 30% + salary increase:	$600	$1,753

It's very likely that events in your life will affect your SR. For example, you will have to take into account the cost of bringing up a child for the entire period from cradle to the first job. One way to take this into account is to use percentages as calculated by statistics organizations in your country. The numbers are very country specific so do your own research. According to Statistics Netherlands, a first child costs about 17% of your household's net income. Two children cost you an average of 26%, three children 33%. These are percentages and therefore regardless of the amount of income. Or if you want to calculate with numbers, you can probably find the average amounts for your country at the relevant statistics or budgeting organizations websites.

For the situation in the Netherlands you can calculate with an average of €4,500 per child per year. In total, a child costs an average of €100,000 from 0 to 22 years of age, including completion of a four-year course of higher education. In the UK the cost of raising a child to the age of 21 has jumped up to GBP 230,000. According to a 2017 report from the U.S. Department of Agriculture, the average cost of raising a child in the United States from birth through age 17 is $233,610. Note that there are huge differences between countries, between regions and between urban versus rural locations.

These absolute amounts are averages. And because the average family does not exist, these indications are too high for some and too low for others. Estimate your own situation based on the percentages and your lifestyle.

If you have passive income in addition to your work, such as renting out a house, you will keep this income after the moment you stop working. You need less money to cover your expenses, so you have a lower FIRE target.

If you stop working voluntarily you cannot count on a contribution from the government in most countries. However, from the moment of retirement you will receive what you are entitled to. If by that time state pension schemes still exists and you have saved up a pension during your working life, you will receive it from your retirement age and this income will cover (part of) your expenses. This means that you do not need to use or build up FIRE capital for this purpose.

FIRE scenarios

I sketch out a few scenarios and substantiate them with figures to show how, for many people, a FIRE target can be achieved more easily or sooner than can be imagined based on the 4% rule of thumb.

These example scenarios are purely to illustrate what is possible for people in different situations. I sketch out scenarios for a single person, a couple without children, a couple with children, a couple with children who have already left home. These are young people who still have all the time they need but also older people who can't save many years but want to stop working early anyway and want to pull their money out from the illiquid assets of their home.

I want to show with the scenarios what the effect is of certain choices on your FIRE goal, on the time you need to save and and on the amount or the SR percentage that needs to be saved to reach your FIRE goal:

- The difference between starting with an SR of 20% and an SR of 30%.
- Taking into account an inheritance to be received
- Decide that you can use all your assets and deplete your FIRE funds
- Decide that you want to get your money out of your house i.e. sell your paid off house and live somewhere cheaper or take out a so-called reverse mortgage.
- Decide that you will add a large part of any future salary increase to your savings (instead of spending it).
- Decide that you will start saving the money you now spend on your children growing up, right from the moment they are financially independent.

Here I explain in words what is happening and what is possible. The tables with all figures you can find online on the tools page. Just think of these numbers in your own currency.

The tables with all the numbers are online at https://fymfire.com/en/tools.

Scenario 1

A single man, 27 years old, has a disposable income of $2,400 pm. He lives in a rental property. He starts with 20% SR and increases this by adding 60% of each salary increase to the monthly savings amount. The net salary increases 2.5% yearly on average. He expects an inheritance of 50K sometime in the next thirty years and at that time adds this in full to his FIRE fund. There is no need to leave money because this scenario does not take into account a partner and children. The idea is to see if it is possible to save 25 years and stop working at the age of 52. This person expects a pension from the age of 67.

The FIRE target amount based on the 4% rule of thumb is calculated: $2,400 minus $480 (20% SR) is $1,920, times 12 months x 25 (rule of thumb) is $576,000. In order to save the target amount with $480 a month, you will have to save 1200 months, or 100 years, if you do not take interest into account. A bit more than 40 years if you calculate with 4% interest.

According to a scenario calculation the following is feasible:

- The salary increases every year by 2.5%, from $2,400 in year 1 to $4,341 in year 25. By adding 60% of each salary increase to the savings amount, the savings amount increases from $480 (20% SR) in year 1 to $1,644 (SR 38%) in year 25.
- The part of the income to be spent increases by a maximum of 1.6% per year from $1,920 in year 1 to $2,696 in year 25.
- With this savings plan and an average return of 4% per year, this person creates a FIRE fund of $455,539 up until year 25.
- This allows a monthly amount of $2,696 that can be spent monthly in year 51 to be withdrawn during the 15 years from FI until pension while no longer working. (The amount actually increases with 1% inflation each year).
- From retirement age there is still enough money left over to draw around $1,000 each month for ten years as a supplement to the pension. Then it's all gone.

If an inheritance of $50,000 is released, for example in year 51, this means 13 more years to supplement the pension or increase the amount to be withdrawn.

If the same person is able to start with an SR of 30% instead of 20% and the same strategy is followed, this results in a FIRE fund of $575,479, approximately $120,000 more. From this capital, for example, $2456 per month can be withdrawn for 35 years (at 4% return on principal).

Scenario 2

A couple, the oldest of the two is 32 years old, wants to find out if it is possible to stop working at the age of 50. Together they have one and a half job and earn $3,600 a month in total. They save 30%.

The calculated FIRE number using the rule of thumb is $756,000. With a savings amount of $1,080 (3,600 x 30%) it will take 700 months (58 years) to reach this goal or 30 years with 4% interest.

They let the SR grow by adding 50% of each salary increase to their savings. They live in their owned house with a current value of $250,000 and they are able to pay off the mortgage in full, in addition to the monthly savings, before the desired FI age after 18 years.

- The income increases during the 18 years from $3,600 to $5,477 and the savings amount rises from $1,080 (SR 30%) to 2019 (37%).
- The amount that can be freely spent increases from $2,520 to $3,458 by 2% per year. They build up assets worth $449,690 up until year 18.
- The moment of FI coincides with the complete pay off of their house, which in the meantime has increased in value from $250,000 to $506,454.
- Because they no longer have to pay mortgage and interest, they decide to draw 75% of the spending level in year 18. They can afford this for 18 years and then the FIRE fund is depleted. This is one year after retirement date.
- The couple decides to liquidate their home to free up that money. At that moment the house is worth almost $950,000. They can generously provide themselves with a supplement to the pension up to the age of 95.

Scenario 3

A couple, age 42, with 2 children (both 15 years old) and 2 jobs. They earn a net total of $4,500 per month. Of this they only save around 10% in the first years but as soon as the children are independent in year 7 they can save the money they have left and their SR rises to 38% in year 13. Whatever the amounts they count on they calculate a FIRE target higher than $1 million. And they certainly don't have enough years to save that.

- They already have assets of $50.000 in year 1 and by saving and a welcome inheritance in year 13 of $100.000 this asset grows to $433.868.
- They stop working and withdraw the same amount as before FI. They can withdraw this amount for 11 years and then it is all gone.
- They liquidate their home and can continue to withdraw the inflation-adjusted amount from the proceeds up to the age of 90.

Scenario 4

A somewhat older couple, age 50, with one job, a net income of $4,000 per month, liquid assets worth $25,000 and a nearly paid off home worth $450,000 in year 1. The children are independent and now the couple can save money, starting with 40% SR.

- They have only 7 years left to work and in that period of time they build up a capital of $202,667.
- From year 8 when they stop working they lower their spending level and withdraw 75% from their FIRE fund of what they are used to.
- They can only do this for 9 years and then the fund is empty.
- Their home is now worth $810,424 and they decide to sell the house or take out a reverse mortgage to pull the money out.
- They apply a 4% Withdrawal Rate and withdraw 4% each year from their assets which average a yield of around 4%.
- The principal is largely maintained, and they leave that to their children.

Scenario 5

A couple, age 30, 2 young children, living in a rented house, with one job and an income of $2,400. The first 22 years they do not save much because the children eat a large part of the disposable income.

The two children cost around $750 per month in year 1 and that increases to over $1,000 per month in the last year the kids are financially dependent on their parents, 22 years later. Still, in 22 years time this couple manages to increase the SR from 6.9% to 24% by adding 50% of each salary increase to the savings amount. Then the children are independent and they start a final sprint by putting all the money that the children normally cost directly into the savings account.

- In 27 years they manage to build up a FIRE fund of $374.388. This is about half of the FIRE target amount based on the 4% rule of thumb.
- They stop working and pay themselves drawing from this capital for 10 years around $2,400 per month.
- At the age of 67 they receive pension and pay themselves a supplement to the pension of $1,000 per month.
- They can do this until the age of 87. Then the money is finished.

I very much hope that the above scenarios give an idea of how I think this can be done in situations where the calculation with the 4% rule of thumb is not hopeful or even dissuasive. No prediction of the future will be correct. No scenario will come true. That's not the purpose of working with and thinking in scenarios.

"The best way to predict your future is to create it."
Abraham Lincoln

What are you going to do?

You've drawn a picture of what you want and you've written down what your life looks like when it all goes according to plan. You have also outlined your ambition for the coming years until you have reached your FYM or FIRE goal. Finally, you have drawn a picture of what your life looks like when you are free to do what you want. The questions in the 'What' phase are about what you are going to do to get there.

Think about what matters to you. Set your goals and design your lifestyle. Think about, and capture, the ideas you want to apply and what changes you want to make to achieve a more conscious life.

When creating FYM and FIRE we often talk about a totally different lifestyle and behavior. The first question is: What behavior is part of your ambitions? For many people it is difficult to sharply formulate the desired behavior. You quickly tend not to focus on defining a behavior but on a result. A simple way to test whether you have formulated the desired behavior clearly enough is to ask the following question several times: What are you going to do?

Look at your abilities, look at your ambitions, and ask yourself:

What do I have to do to realize my ambition?

What should I do for Get: Generate income?

What should I do for Keep: Not spend all my money?

What should I do for Grow: Saving & Investing?

What should I do for Achieve: Comfortable FI life?

Which actions do I need to perform regularly from now on?

What else should I do? What should I do less? What should I learn?

Think of as many behaviors as possible. Also look at how other people achieve goals.

Capture this in your documentation.

Financial targets

Determine financial objectives for all four strategies Get, Keep, Grow and Achieve.

Get

Generating income - how much do I earn; how much can I grow my income?

Keep

Save - how much do I spend (Burn Rate), how much do I save (Savings Rate), how fast do I think I can lower my Burn Rate and increase my Savings Rate? What is my ultimate Savings Rate?

Grow

Savings & Investments - how much am I going to save and invest in what form, how much return do I expect? How about risk?

Achieve

Comfortable FI life - how much money do I need, what amounts are my
FYM goals or FIRE goal? How much money do I want to be able to withdraw (Withdrawal Rate) and spend (Burn Rate)? When do I think I will be able to reach my goals based on my estimation of savings, investments and FYM/FIRE goals?

Capture this in your documentation.

Part 3

How

'Voluntary simplicity means
going fewer places in one day rather than more,
seeing less so I can see more,
doing less so I can do more,
acquiring less so I can have more.'

John Kabat-Zinn, American molecular biologist and founder of the

Stress Reduction Clinic

Chapter 10
How to do it

The next step is 'How', doing, action. You start with Get, Keep, Grow. Not all immediately and not all at the same time. You are going to create your FYM or FIRE fund, or both. You are going to create Financial Independence and you can start immediately.

How do we get to our goal, whatever the goal is?

'95% of the people give up on their goals right before they are about to hit them. Be the other 5%.'
Kyle Weiger, handstand coach

From Good To Great applied

I apply some lessons from Jim Collins' book 'From Good to Great' to our journey and search for more freedom and Financial Independence.

Define a set of core values aimed at a higher goal than simply saving money or achieving FIRE. Think also about ikigai and Jim Collins' sweet spot. Imagine having a Big Hairy Audacious Goal (BHAG). This is a goal that is concrete and ambitious enough to guide your progress for years to come. When do you want to achieve and do something?

Commit to a long marathon that brings you to your BHAG: commit to your daily actions to eventually reach your long-term goals. It's better to consistently do something that delivers results than to perform spectacularly one moment and be weak the next.

Do your thing smarter and better than anyone else. Take the following steps to speed up this process.

- Determine what you can be the best at but also what you can't be the best at. Can you somehow make more money easier, can you save money or invest money? Can you beat the market and professional investors, or will you stick to a limited-risk investment strategy?
- Determine what drives you financially. What do you want to achieve? What do you want to build a FYM or FIRE fund for?
- Determine what you are passionate about. And spend more time and attention to that.

Stick to your criteria, avoid being distracted by things that are not really important to you personally.

Confront the Brutal Facts: look as honestly as possible at the facts and figures and do this regularly. You must remain unbreakable in believing that you can and will prevail in the end, regardless of the difficulties you may face, and at the same time have the discipline to confront the most brutal facts of your present reality, whatever they may be. I find the insight I gain by looking at my expenses in a structured way both confronting (sometimes) and helpful (mostly).

Set up a 'Stop Doing' list. That's like a To Do list but the other way around. And then stop everything that is not in line with your ambitions, and that does not deliver the value you desire.

Jim Collins, Good to Great:
Why Some Companies Make the Leap...And Others Don't

How to become 'effective': seven habits of highly effective people

We all have our dreams and ambitions and we all want to succeed. One of the paths to success is to identify 'habits' that can help us on our journey. In Stephen Covey's book 'The 7 Habits of Highly Effective People' the author speaks of the following seven habits:

1. Be proactive
2. Begin with the end in mind
3. Put first things first
4. Think Win-Win
5. First seek to understand, then to be understood
6. Synergize
7. Sharpen the saw

The first reason why I find the book 'The Seven Habits' interesting and relevant is the explanation that so many people who appear to have achieved success are still struggling with an inner need to develop personal effectiveness. In the context of FIRE, I am thinking about people who receive quite a substantial income but are totally ineffective at saving.

We see the world entirely based on our own perceptions. What is right for one is wrong for the other. What is successful for one (the top job), the other sees as stress (the same job). In order not to make our journey of FYM and FIRE too difficult, we simply have to change our buying behavior and spending pattern. However, to be able to do this, we need to change ourselves and our lifestyle, we need to change our perception of what we find important and what we find bullshit.

Habit 1: Be proactive

I feel privileged and have been lucky at times. I also strongly believe that success is not only the result of chance but also of making choices, of doing something or not doing something and of actions which follow those choices.

Covey describes it perhaps even more clearly, he says:

> *"We are in charge. We choose the scripts ourselves with which we live our lives. You have to be aware of this, be proactive and take responsibility for your choices."*

Reactive people take a passive attitude, they believe the world is happening to them. They say things like: 'There's nothing I can do. That's just the way I am.' They think that the problem is 'out there' - for example, the job market is bad, my family expects a lot from me, my friends have a certain opinion about me - but this thought is the problem. Reactivity becomes a self-fulfilling prophecy, and reactive people feel increasingly victimized. Many people think that creating FYM or achieving FI is not for them but this is exactly what Covey means by a reactive attitude that will prove itself because reactive people don't do anything for it.

However, proactive people recognize that they have responsibility - or "responsiveness," which Covey defines as the ability to choose how to respond to a particular stimulus or situation.

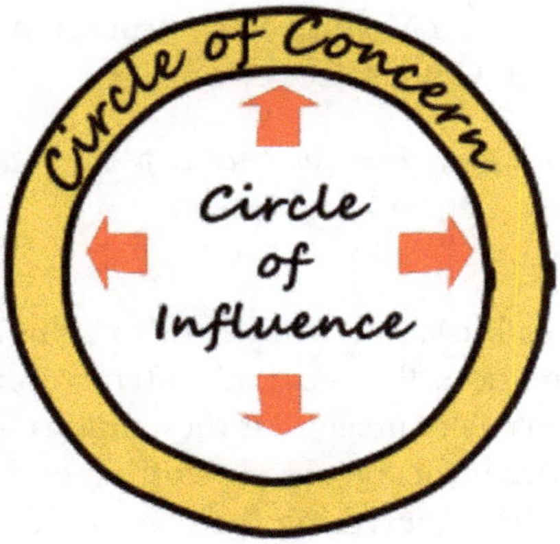

To be proactive, we need to focus on the Circle of Influence that lies within our Circle of Concern. To what extent do I commit myself, what do I spend my time on, what is my level of experience, what skills do I have, what do I learn? In other words; we have to work on the things we can do something about. You'll see that the energy we exert on the things in our Circle of Influence will only make our Circle of Influence grow bigger.

Proactive focus: You spend most of your time and energy changing what you can change. Your life improves and you stop blaming others. You increase your circle of influence with positive energy

Reactive people, on the other hand, concentrate on things that fall within their Circle of Concern but not within their Circle of Influence, which leads to putting blame on external factors, radiating negative energy, and causing a shrinking Circle of Influence.

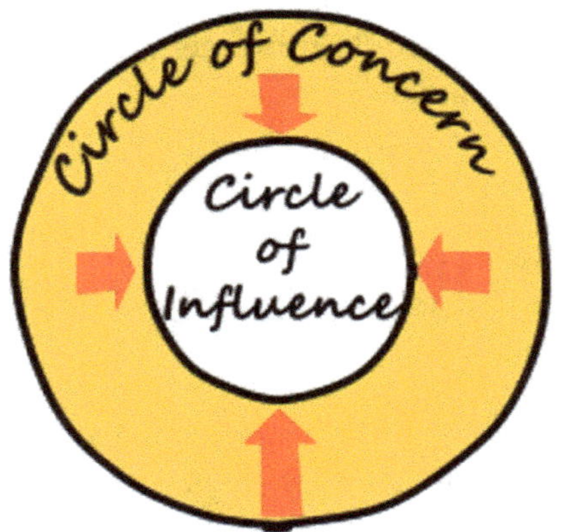

Reactive focus: You focus your time and energy on worries and problems. You do not take responsibility for your own situation. You reduce your circle of influence with negative energy.

These are all great life lessons. And I would like to emphasize that in your FYM and FIRE journey you should also focus on things you can influence and not pay too much (or actually no) attention to what happens outside your 'Circle of Influence'. Don't care too much about what others think about your new behavior deviating from the norm.

As far as I am concerned, if you are reactive and stay reactive, you don't have to enter into a conversation with yourself in thirty years' time, 'I wish I had...'.

Habit 2: Begin with the end in mind

I have already talked at length about the importance of dreams. It's so important that you first consider why you started the journey of FYM and FIRE. I mentioned earlier the Big Hairy Audacious Goal (BHAG) of Jim Collins. Covey calls it:

"Start with a clear destiny in mind, you can use your imagination to develop a vision of what you want to become and you can use your consciousness to decide what values will guide us."

We generally find it quite easy to keep ourselves busy. We work hard to achieve successes, promotions, higher income, more recognition. But we don't often stop to evaluate the meaning behind these victories, we don't ask ourselves if these things we focus on are really important to us. We don't wonder if this rat race is worth it and is going in the right direction, if this hamster wheel life is everything there is and if we can ever get rid of our lifestyle creep or get sucked deeper and deeper into it.

'It's incredibly easy to get caught up in an activity trap, in the busyness of life, to work harder and harder at climbing the ladder to success only to discover that it's leaning against the wrong wall.'
Stephen Covey

Habit 2 suggests that in everything we do, we should start with the end in mind. Start with a clear destiny. In this way we can ensure that the steps we take go in the right direction, and it motivates us to actually take them.

Calculating how much money you need for your dream and determining when you can save this amount is an inspiring goal for many of us. Having such concrete goals keeps us focused.

Covey emphasizes that our self-awareness enables us to shape our own lives, rather than living a standard life or a life based on the standards or preferences of others. How powerful do you feel this is!

Habits 3: Put first things first

To manage ourselves effectively, we have to put the first things, the most important things, first. In our FYM and FIRE journey, we must not lose ourselves in futile pursuits but we must have the discipline to prioritize our actions based on what we ourselves find most important, not what is most urgent (or what others find important).

In Habit 2 we discussed the importance of defining our values and understanding what we want to achieve. Habits 3 is about actually pursuing these goals and executing our priorities from day to day, moment to moment.

In order to maintain the discipline and focus to stay on track towards our goals, we need the willpower to do something, even if we don't want to do a certain essential and sensible thing. Or we must refrain from doing or buying something, even if we feel a strong desire to do or own it. We have to act consciously and intentionally according to our values instead of our desires or impulses. The challenge is not to manage our time but to manage ourselves. All activities can be subdivided on the basis of two factors: urgent and important.

Take a look at this time management matrix (and if you weren't familiar with this matrix yet, start using it often):

	Urgent	Not urgent
Important	Quadrant 1 Crisis Deadline-driven projects Urgent problem	Quadrant 2 Building relationships Plans Recognizing new possibilities
Not important	Quadrant 3 Interruptions Some (or many) phone calls and meetings Popular activities	Quadrant 4 Nonsensical tasks Occupational therapy Fun things Work avoidance behavior

We often respond to urgent matters and spend most of our time there on things that are not always important. In our attempt to learn a conscious and somewhat frugal lifestyle, we need to hold back and not respond to impulses, we need to plan a little more so that we don't have to buy things last minute. By saving and putting aside enough money every month, we avoid having to put time and energy into solving crises and problems, which only leads to stress, burn-out and constantly extinguishing of fires.

When we spend most of our time responding to things that seem urgent, while the reality is that their urgency is based on the priorities and expectations of others, it leads to short-term focus, a sense of loss of control and distraction from our goal. A lot of these activities you do because of FOMO.

In order to spend our time on the important things only, we need to learn how to say 'no' to other activities, which sometimes seem urgent but are not important. Remember the Joy of Missing Out.

Habits 4: Think Win-Win

Covey speaks of win-win situations between people. This habit appeals to me mainly because I think it's important for the feasibility of our FYM and FIRE plans that we look for the win-win-win combination of Smarter, Better, Cheaper. I don't think it is necessary to become too frugal and to me it is not at all the idea of FYM and FIRE that you have to abstain yourself from all the pleasures of life, temporarily or otherwise.

The best option is to create win-win situations. The idea or solution should be mutually beneficial, mutually satisfying. Win-win is a belief in the third alternative. It is not cheaper ór better but it is smarter, cheaper and better.

With win-lose or lose-win you have to sacrifice too much to save on something, or you have to accept too much loss of quality if you can't really pay for something. Or one person currently gets what he wants but the partner feels that too much is sacrificed.

The 'win-win or no-deal' option is important to use as a backup. Having No Deal as an option in your mind frees you from the need to manipulate yourself or someone else. It prevents us from feeling compelled (by ourselves or by someone else) to do something.

Habit 5: Seek first to understand, then to be understood.

Before we can give advice, suggest solutions or communicate effectively with someone else in any way, we must try to understand the other person and his or her perspective through empathetic listening. Whether or not it is important to you that others understand you and the concepts of FYM and FIRE depends on whether you have a partner with whom you want to share the journey. Or it depends on you wanting your friends to understand and accept your behavior because they understand the goals you want to achieve. By first understanding the other you prevent someone feeling manipulated by you, because if that happens, he or she will question your motives and stop opening up.

My experience is that there are many people (including my partner) who at first did not understand me and my choices. What I have had to learn is to understand the other first. If the other person thinks life is going to be meagre and paltry and that it is all going to be about saving money all the time, I will have to spend time and attention on understanding this first and only then explaining better what I mean. According to Covey:

> *If we can present our ideas clearly, and in the context of a deep understanding of the needs and concerns of the other, we significantly increase the credibility of our ideas'.*

Habits 6: Synergize

By understanding and appreciating the differences in another person's perspective, we have the ability to create synergy, allowing us to discover new possibilities through openness and creativity. It's about searching together for and coming up with creative opportunities to generate extra income, to save extra money or even to set more easily achievable goals, so that you can reach your FYM or FIRE goal sooner. When we become aware of someone's different perspective, we can say: 'Good! You see it differently! Help me see what you see.'

Next time you disagree with your partner, with whom you are walking your FYM and FIRE path, try to understand his or her point of view first. The better you understand him or her, the easier it will be for your partner to change his or her mind, of for you to change yours, and find synergy.

Habit 7: Sharpen the saw

Habit 7 is aimed at renewal or taking the time to sharpen the saw (and to not saw harder and longer with a blunt saw). To be effective, we need to spend time on the physical, spiritual, mental and social renewal of ourselves. I find achieving and maintaining balance very important in our FYM and FIRE journey. You can't just work harder and spend less to maximize your Savings Rate. You have to keep taking care of yourself, otherwise you can't keep it up in the long run. People generally overestimate what they can do in one day and underestimate what they can do in their entire lives. FYM and FIRE are not short sprints but with enough patience a lot is possible.

Stephen R. Covey,
The 7 Habits of Highly Effective People (2010)

Keep it fun, make it easy

Keeping the process fun sometimes seems like a difficult part of your journey but I do think you can make your journey fun. I have experienced that gamification works well for me. During my travels the lowering of my 'average spending per day' has a reverse positive effect on my metric 'total number of travel days'. The 'total number of travel days' mainly serves a motivating purpose and has no real predictive value at all.

Celebrate your successes. Long-term goals have no daily successes. Think of milestones and celebrate the successful achievement of those milestones. You can do this by celebrating the achievement of an X% of your FI number, the achievement of a certain Savings Rate during a month, the repayment of an X% of your mortgage, et cetera.

I'd also like to advise you to try to cut the ambitions that seem difficult to achieve into smaller steps and turn them into habits. BJ Fogg has a whole book dedicated to what he calls Tiny Habits. He states that creating habits and positive change can be easy, if you have the right approach.

We know that habits matter and play an important part of our lives. We just need more good habits and less bad ones. And yet we struggle to change and blame ourselves for it.

According to BJ Fogg you have to do three things to develop successful habits and change your behavior:

- Stop judging yourself.
- Take your ambitions and divide them into small behaviors.
- Embrace mistakes as discoveries and use them to move on.

The essence of Tiny Habits is this: take a behavior you aspire to, make it small, find where it naturally fits into your life and cherish its growth. If you want to create change in the long run, it's best to start small. And this is why:

Tiny is fast

We believe there will never be enough time. We say no to change because we feel we don't have the time to develop new positive habits. Thirty minutes of exercise a day? Start with 10 push-ups. Cook a healthy dinner every night? Start with one home cooked serving of vegetables with each meal. You can make your life a lot easier. You can start small.

Tiny can start now

No More Apologies!

Tiny feels safe

It can be difficult, scary or even unsafe to start something new if it's too big.

Tiny can become big

We find it difficult to identify or even accept small improvements. People become frustrated and demoralized when things don't happen quickly. A small action may feel insignificant at first but it allows you to get the momentum you need to take on bigger challenges and make progress. Every euro or dollar you don't spend but save is one in the right direction!

Tiny doesn't rely on motivation or willpower

As you know, motivation and willpower get a lot of attention. The problem is that both motivation and willpower are unreliable. Keeping changes small and expectations low is how to design around motivation and willpower. If something is small, it is easy to do, which means you do not have to rely on the unreliable nature of motivation or willpower.

Tiny is transformational

With the Tiny Habits method, you celebrate your successes, no matter how small they may be. When we feel successful, we can learn new habits, and it motivates us to do more.

BJ Fogg, Tiny Habits,
The Small Changes That Change Everything (2019)

Don't make it too big: the basics of FIRE investing

It seems that investing is a big thing for many people. We can use this as a good example of how you can make it tiny and manageable. You can start right away by creating your personal FIRE jar. There are all kinds of small steps that, as long as it doesn't cost any money, can be easily reversed. You can open the accounts you need; deposit the money you have not spent and buy your first ETF. My advice here is mainly K.I.S.S. (Keep It Simple Stupid).

You don't have to make a study out of it but first read on. I'm going to explain as many aspects of FIRE investing as possible, in 'Grow: How do I grow my money'.

It is widely accepted in the international FIRE communities that you build up a portfolio of mainly very widely spread index funds (preferably ETFs), with a relatively low risk that you buy at the lowest transaction costs. This already feels a lot less scary, doesn't it?

In addition, it is a rule of thumb that you buy small quantities of the ETF over time with great regularity. You're really in it for the long term and therefore it is strongly inadvisable to wait for a good entry moment, just start right away and regularly deposit small amounts. Tiny!

What you also shouldn't do is try to beat the market. The advice I would like to give you at this stage, and many FIRE adepts are with me on this is: don't try to time the market and don't buy specific shares or less widely spread funds. Years of studies, many articles and many experts all say the same thing: you're not going to succeed anyway. Even Warren Buffet has been heard saying: "index funds are 'the most sensible equity investment' for most people". So, unless you really think you know better than 'most people' you'd better accept this.

Experiment

Start by experimenting. You're going for it, and this means that you don't have to apply all your ideas at once, do what feels right. Try a month of not buying anything, introduce No-Spend-Days, don't use a car for a month. Don't go out for a month, prepare your own food and invite people to join you. See what happens, what feels good and what doesn't. You run a big risk that if it's all going very well and you like it so much that you might want to go further in getting rid of stuff or consuming less. You might want to experiment more and come up with excellent creative solutions to the practical problems you are confronted with. You also run the risk that your new lifestyle will feel better, 'lighter' is what people often describe. You will probably find that for many things Smarter, Better, Cheaper is possible. Win-win-win.

Sometimes the best way to find out what you don’t need comes from involuntary and unplanned situations. Years ago, living in Amsterdam and London my wife and I owned cars and motorcycles. From the moment we live in Goa we haven’t had any means of transportation. We walked everywhere, every day. Our daily walk to buy essential groceries became a habit. We tried different routes, got to know the neighborhood well and found more local stores where we bought bread, vegetables or fruit. When we didn't necessarily need anything we walked through the jungle, crossed old bridges over the river or walked a little further away to end up on a completely empty beach with palm trees. It became part of our routine and we found that it keeps us mentally and physically fit.

It is now a conscious choice not to have a means of transportation and if absolutely necessary we can go somewhere by cab or rikshaw or rent a car, scooter or motorcycle for one day. Not renting the scooter saves us money every day, on our daily average budget it saves about 20%. From the money of one day's scooter rental we can buy 16 pounds of fresh vegetables, or 6 pounds of fruit or twenty days fresh bread rolls for lunch.

I think this is a nice example of Smarter, Better, Cheaper. This is also a nice example of happenstance. Whereas happenstance is coincidental, I believe you can stimulate this to happen by changing your circumstances and allowing things to happen. That's why I advise you to experiment and force yourself not to use a certain item for a month, or not to do a certain activity for a month. Try this with something that has no real noticeable day-to-day cost and which you know it is not really giving you a lot of value, pleasure or happiness. Probably your main motivation only comes from convenience?

Don't use your car for a month or don't buy any coffee to go for a month. Don't buy any new clothes for six months. Change a paid service like Spotify premium to the free version. How do you feel about it? What are you going to do differently? Have you found a solution to an inconvenience? Have you discovered something new?

Experiment with No-Spend-Days. How hard is it to go through a day without spending any money at all? What do you need to prepare to spend no money at all during the week? What about weekends? And if you don't spend a single dime for two days in a row? And three? What happens to your week total spending? Do you still buy the things you actually wanted on the other days, or do you end up spending less, for example because you've put more thought into your shopping needs?

Experiment with cord cutting. Ditch cable and don't watch television for a whole week or month. Are you able to follow everything that is important to you over the internet? What do you do with the time you normally spend watching television? Do you fill in this time with something valuable? Experiment with No-Digital-days, a whole day (or more) not online. Does it give you peace of mind or do you keep worrying about what you might be missing? Do you feel that you need to account to others for your online absence? Or are you able to plan it all well and does it actually work?

Experiment with Do It Yourself gym. Cancel your membership. If the DIY experiment is not successful, you can easily shop around and compare different gyms. But first try to be active or exercise as much as possible on your own for a month. Can you add a short workout to your routine in the morning, at home, possibly with some free exercise videos to motivate yourself? Can you take an extra walk a couple of times a week, for at least one hour, around your house, different routes? Can you do something physically active in the park, forest or on the beach that makes you happy or relaxed?

Create your own experiments for things in your life that you doubt are really important or which you already second guessed the added value of, or something of which you doubt whether the costs are unreasonably high compared to the benefits. Think of 'The Good Life' and ikigai again and consider what it all brings you.

The goal of all these kinds of experiments is on how you experience doing things differently. Also, you can use the practices from your successful experiments and continue. Think about how you can best convert the experiment into a habit, is there anything you need to do, organize, prepare or buy before you can start the behavioral change?

If you decide never to drink expensive coffee outside again, you might want to equip yourself with the right tools to make a good cup at home. Maybe you should buy a yoga mat to do a short workout or yoga session at home more often? Maybe you could join the library so you can read some magazines regularly there because you could cancel all your magazine subscriptions? Maybe you should buy an e-reader or start using yours more, so you can get rid of all your books and even get rid of your bookcase. Maybe you never need to buy a physical book again and from now on you will only borrow books and e-books from friends and from the library?

The goal of experimenting is not to deny yourself everything and not be able to enjoy anything from now on. The goal is to enjoy and do things smarter while reducing your expenses - Smarter, Better, Cheaper - and have more money left at the end of the month.

What does your action plan look like?

It feels good to know how much money you need to temporarily not work, or never work again at all, until when you need to make money, how much money you need to make, how much your investments will or should return. But unfortunately, that's not how life works. You can't plan everything.

With diving I learned: Plan your dive (so you know how long you can stay at what depth with your amount of air) and Dive your plan (so you don't run out of air). In practice, however, it turns out that your dive does not resemble your plan at all, that there are all kinds of reasons to deviate from your plan, that circumstances turn out to be different from what you assumed when planning. And nowadays we have dive computers that tell us how long we have been underwater, how deep we have been and, to the nearest minute, how long we can stay at a certain depth. Supplemented with a meter that indicates how much air we have left, I can completely adjust my dive while diving, for example, I can swim less deep and thus increase my maximum dive time considerably.

I use this as a metaphor with FYM and FIRE. If you have financial windfalls during your working life, you are more likely to reach FI. If your investments do better than you thought, you will reach your FIRE goal sooner. If you spend less FYM than budgeted on a wonderful trip, you can take extend the trip or keep the remainder and put it back in your FYM fund. My point is, you have to be a bit flexible with Get, Keep, Grow and Achieve.

And you have to dare to take the first step. 'Every journey of 1000 miles starts with a first step' (Lao Tzu). Taking that first step is not that difficult at all. Once you have formulated the ambitions and behavioral change you want to achieve, you are already ahead of most people who are trying to change something in their lives.

Now it is time for more concrete steps. I would like to suggest a simple way of planning actions. The time period of a month is arbitrary, so choose your own period. If you are working fulltime right now, formulating a list of actions for a month is fine.

If you are not working at the moment and have all the time to do it full time, I advise you to make the lists below on a weekly basis.

Before formulating your action plan, it might be useful to first continue reading a little further and not literally start drawing up your complete action plan right away. At the same time, I warn you to not wait too long. After all some things you can start right now.

Let's get to work! Good luck!

Formulate a number of warm-up actions

First formulate a number of actions that you can do to 'warm up', specify when you are going to perform these actions, the next days or week. These are literally simple actions that you can perform as soon as you have a few minutes of time. For example, you can directly convert your Spotify account to a free subscription, you can directly apply for memberships (library?) or cancel expensive memberships or subscriptions (gym?). You can find out directly at your current bank what an investment account costs, and if it is free, open it immediately.

Now think about all the actions you can do in the coming month to really get started and realize your formulated ambitions?

Get actions 1st month: Generate income

Keep actions 1st month: Not spending all that comes in

Grow actions 1st month: Save & invest

Achieve actions 1st month: Harvest, Withdraw

Finally, write down the actions you already have in mind but cannot take in the first month, for whatever reason. These actions are your Backlog, a list of actions to be performed later.

Backlog for **Get**: Generate income

Backlog for **Keep**: Not spending all that comes in

Backlog for **Grow**: Save & invest

Backlog for **Achieve**: Harvest, Withdraw

The next month, while you are performing the first actions, you can complete these backlog lists with actions that come to mind. In one month you will be finished with the actions of the first month and the actions that didn't succeed will be added to your backlog.

Beginning of month 2:

Grab your 1st month action lists, add the outstanding actions to your backlog and start prioritizing: organize the list so that the most important and/or urgent items are at the top.

Now pick up the actions at the top first and copy them to your 2nd month action lists to create.

Get started with this and fill your backlog with actions that occur to you during the month.

This method, if it works for you, can be repeated every month. You will see that there will be fewer and fewer actions.

Tip:
There are apps available for your smartphone (free) in which you can create and maintain action lists. I've been using Microsoft To Do. The app syncs with the cloud and my other devices like my iPad and laptop. The app also shares and syncs certain action lists with my wife. Try one or more apps.
Since you have started with a productivity hack (the action lists/to do app) make it a habit to write down everything you think you should or want to do in that app.

Evaluate & Adjust: Measuring progress, doing reviews and adjusting your working method

The last part of the step 'How' in this approach is 'Evaluating & Adapting'. What went well, what can be done better or differently? Can you enjoy more by spending less? Do you feel you are on the right track? Which goals can you set higher or lower? Introduce new experiments or determine that from now on this is how you do it. Monitor your progress and celebrate your successes.

But also: How do you deal with something that doesn't work or isn't fun? I advise you to regularly ask yourself if it works, how well it works, and if you should deal with it in a different way. Also with something like a change in lifestyle and the accompanying behavioral changes it is important to monitor your behavior.

Start by carefully keeping track of whether you have fulfilled your behavioral intentions. You can do this by making a note, and capture, whether you are really making progress. Your action lists will also show if you have made progress. I use Google Keep for making these kinds of notes, both on my phone and laptop but any note app is useful.

From the second month you can do a short weekly review with yourself by looking back and looking forward and improving your structure and planning. If you don't feel like you have so much to review every week after a couple of months, it's fine to take some time once a month for a monthly review.

A final tip I often come across in productivity articles and podcasts is to find a buddy or accountability partner to do the weekly or monthly reviews with. It's inspiring to have someone you can discuss this topic with, who understands you and can help you in your journey. What you are doing is not inspiring for everyone and many people won't understand you, but that doesn't matter in the end. It is just nice if there is at least one person you can use as a sparring partner.

Who do you tell

It can be helpful in realizing your dreams and in adjusting your behavior to share with others what you are doing, why and where you want to go. Depending on your situation you will have to do this tactically. It will not be perceived positively by every employer if he gets the feeling that you want to quit your job as soon as possible and that until that time you just want to earn as much FYM as possible.

Sharing your dreams and plans privately is pleasant in a small circle. However, it is not recommended to be too explicit about how much money exactly you are talking about. If you save on luxury, abstain from all sorts of things, have a side hustle to make some extra money and put a lot of effort into creating a FIRE fund of a few hundred thousand, there might be people who don't understand your behavior. They don't like the idea or the concept or perhaps they suddenly turn out to be your best friend and come to you to borrow money.

Sharing your dreams, ambitions and even the issues you encounter with friends or family along the way is helpful and important but becoming too specific can cause adverse effects.

Chapter 11
Get: Make Money

Unless you receive an inheritance or win the lottery (and I personally don't advise you to spend money on buying lottery tickets as the chances of achieving your goals that way is extremely small), you will first need to generate income to work on Financial Independence.

Working for your money

Whether you are employed by a company, by the government or self-employed, it is worthwhile to think about how you can increase your income.

What can you do to increase your income?

- Can you invest in yourself by taking lessons or a course to learn specific skills or knowledge?
- Can you talk to your manager to discuss a pay rise?
- Can you do something that will make you more valuable to the company?
- Can you look for a job in another department or even at another company to increase your value and increase your salary?
- Can you consider a completely different career and corresponding salary, do you need retraining for this?
- Can you start working for yourself?
- In addition to your job, can you do other paid work, additional jobs?

Dare to negotiate. This, for most people, is not pleasant and not easy but it can be worth it. Realize that if you negotiate a few percent extra at the beginning of a trajectory, a job or an assignment, it will earn you money for the rest of the time you work. Also keep in mind that for the person you're negotiating with, your employer, manager, recruiter, human resources, client or head of procurement, it's probably quite normal to negotiate. It's part of the job for your interviewer. Make it clear what you think you are worth.

If it is indicated that there is no budget for a higher fee, indicate that you can meet the budget by delivering less, less hours for example, so that you do receive a good fee per hour and also deliver the performance expected of you. And then you have time to do something else.

If it is not possible to negotiate extra salary, you may be able to negotiate fringe benefits. Common fringe benefits are basic items often included in hiring packages. These include health insurance, life insurance, tuition assistance, childcare reimbursement, cafeteria subsidies, below-market loans, employee discounts, employee stock options, and personal use of a company-owned vehicle.

Think about what you find important and discuss this. Do you want more free time? It will cost your employer little to give you extra time off or longer unpaid parental leave. Is your employer willing to facilitate sports at work or pay a sports subscription? Would you like to work from home more often? Discuss the possibilities and benefits for you and your employer of working from home more often. Discuss a work from home allowance and a budget for setting up your work place at home. Is it possible that more time and money will be made available for training? Together with your manager, can you draw up a development plan with relevant training and a sufficient budget? Discuss your travel allowance. Is it possible and fiscally advantageous to buy a bicycle? Take a look at your pension plan. What has been arranged and how much is paid in contributions? Is this sufficient or can you negotiate a supplementary pension or an amount that you use for your own old-age provision?

Think of the sweet spot of Collins and ikigai. Become aware of what your passion is and what you are good at in your work. Look for the overlap between the two and consider whether this is what you have been or can be hired for. This is probably where you add most value for your employer or client. This is what you want to be well paid for.

Start working for yourself

Do you have a certain skill that you can make profitable by setting up your own business? Think of selling your services online, tutoring or designing courses. Can you set up a business that markets a specific service? Think of a dog walking service, a design company, a restaurant, a consulting firm or a software company.

I speak from my own experience when I recognize the fact that for many knowledge workers it is especially useful at the beginning of their career to work for a (large) company where everything is well organized, where you get learning, growing and development opportunities, where you can continue to enjoy education and training, where you can make steps up the ladder and learn different responsibilities.

For many knowledge workers, I think there may be a moment in their career where considering to start working for themself might be interesting. My experience is that after almost ten years of employment, from the moment I started working for myself, it became easier for me to focus on only the things that made me, and my clients, happy. It became easier to make money with the things I was good at and to work for clients who appreciate my skills. And instead of seeing the majority of what the client paid for my work going to my employer's bank account, the money now came directly to me. I started earning much more, although I worked less and didn't work full-time. In addition to more money, I got much more freedom and free time in return.

Tip:
In most countries getting a mortgage to buy a house is only possible with a fixed contract or a financially stable business for a long time (banks are not keen on starting entrepreneurs, self-employed people, flexible contracts etcetera). If you think you want to own a house in the future and you are considering going to be self-employed sometime in the future, buy your house first. You can quit your job as soon as you live in your house because you will keep the mortgage.

Side hustles

There are many opportunities to generate extra income with a side job, or side hustle. In recent years, new platforms have emerged in which self-employed workers are hired for chores via websites or apps. Working as a deliveryman, driver (Uber), security guard or babysitter is also a flexible possibility to do extra jobs when it suits you.

Keep in mind that almost all paid activities performed by so-called Digital Nomads are suitable as a side job if you are handy with computers or social media. You can design or test websites from home, work as a translator, blog, vlog or even set up your own web shop and sell things like jewelry, gadgets, clothing or furniture.

It's probably best if you can earn something with what you enjoy doing. Monetizing a hobby or skill isn't always possible in your paid employment. In Collins' model this is not in your sweet spot because your employer doesn't want to pay for it. But you can put it in your sweet spot by finding someone else willing to pay for it. It may be that you can work as a freelancer, or that you want to register as a self-employed person at the Chamber of Commerce. There are successful hobbyists who bake cakes, give cooking workshops, teach painting, prepare meals, take pictures and sell them online, write texts, teach yoga, etcetera.

In certain industries it is very common for an employee to do paid work next to the principal job. See for yourself what is possible. There are plenty of examples of people who, in addition to their job as, for example, accountant or IT employee at a government organization or company, enjoy working in the evening for startups, as an independent agency, contributing to a project as a programmer or working on their own blog and earn money with it.

The most effective is to immediately set aside all income from side hustles and turn it into FYM or FIRE money.

Passive income: renting out your house

It can be interesting, if you have your own house, to rent out part of the house or temporarily the entire house if you do not live there yourself.

For many people the invasion of privacy might be a dealbreaker but you can easily come up with something and make your property more suitable for partial or temporary rental.

The idea that you don't like people using your belongings or sleeping in your bed when you rent out your house during your own vacation can also be easily overcome. First of all, consider that in a hotel you sleep in a bed that thousands of people have used before you and secondly, you can simply buy an extra set of sheets for your guests and stow your private belongings in a locked closet.

You will have to find out what the rules, restrictions and possibilities are in your municipality, city or country but in principle temporary rental of your own home is possible and not too difficult to organize. There are all kinds of companies that can take care of the reception of guests, the cleaning of the house and the check out at the end of their stay if you do not feel like it or are not able to do so yourself.

Tax Plans

Income tax

I'm not a tax consultant and I don't think you need one just yet whilst you're at the beginning of your journey. Much of the more technical details of this subject goes too far for this book but I still want to summarize the essence in my own words. Also, the rules, limitations and possibilities are very different depending on the country you live in, so it makes no sense to go into detail here.

I have made use of certain tax facilities/rules on several occasions and this can help you reach your goal sooner. The simplest tax planning rule is to postpone paying tax on your income: at the moment you make money you save or invest tax-free and only later you withdraw and use this money and pay tax on it.

In the end, you pay less income tax and at a later time by reducing your taxable income at the moment you receive the income and you use the money at a later moment. Your income will probably be lower when you are not working, you are charged a lower tax rate and you pay less tax. In addition, you can invest the money you don't have to pay to the tax authorities now and gain the extra benefit of paying tax (much) later.

The higher your tax bracket, the more tax-efficient this type of investment is. However, you can't use the money for a long time, as in the case of a pension plan/account.

Taxable accounts

A normal savings account or investment account is an example of a taxable account. These accounts do not have tax advantages but they offer fewer restrictions and more flexibility than fiscally advantageous accounts. You can withdraw your money at any time and for any reason without tax or penalty.

Tax advantageous accounts

Tax-advantaged accounts are generally either tax-deferred or tax-exempt. Deferred tax accounts offer a tax benefit in advance. These are generally pension savings or pension investment accounts. You have the option to build up assets directly from your gross income, which means that you do not pay income tax and you do not have to pay any capital gains tax on the assets invested for your pension. The idea is that you pay tax at the moment you start using the money and that you are then in a lower income tax rate group and have to pay less tax. In the US an IRA is an account set up at a financial institution that allows you to save for retirement with tax-free growth or on a tax-deferred basis. Also in the US a 401(k) plan is a tax-advantaged, defined-contribution retirement account offered by many employers to their employees. In the UK an ISA, or Individual Savings Account, is a savings account that you don't pay tax on. These plans and account usually come with one or more restrictions. Such as the amount of money you can save or invest in a single tax year and the age from when you can withdraw your money.

Dividend tax: dividend leakage

Companies pay dividends from profits after tax, which means that the tax authorities have taken their share. As an investor, you do not have to pay dividend tax as well. If you own shares or ETFs in foreign companies from a country where a higher percentage of dividend tax is levied, you may unjustifiably receive less dividend. This is called dividend leakage. This dividend tax leakage especially hurts ETFs and index funds. It is a good idea to find out which ETF does and which ETF does not suffer from this dividend leakage in your country.

Tax on savings and investments: capital gains

You partly avoid capital gains tax by investing part of your assets in pension investments, which are exempt from this tax. In some countries it's very common to make these investments using gross income.

Chapter 12
Keep: Save

The essence of this chapter is: don't spend all your money. This is simply said but not easily done. You have already thought about your desired conscious lifestyle and we have also discussed before that we don't want to turn into a penny-pincher but that we do want to think about how we can achieve a Smarter, Better, Cheaper lifestyle, with smart choices and decisions that lead to a conscious life in which you have money left over to invest.

It is advisable to set up your own system with your own metrics and indicators and your savings goals and opportunities. This will work well when you start experimenting with parts of your new lifestyle and applying ideas, principles and tactics to save money.

I'm not going to come up with the '38 saving tips for a family' or the '115 fantastic saving tips for home'. I have two reasons for this: I want to help you think for yourself and come up with ideas that are relevant and feasible for your situation. There is no one-size-fits-all method. You are better off creating your personal approach that works best for your situation. The second reason is that there are plenty of books and blogs that share all kinds of tips, 'Google is your friend'.

Just enough

Earlier I mentioned that we do and buy a lot of the things under social pressure. Now that we are looking at where we can save money, it makes sense to think about what is enough. Look for this optimum, not too much but also not too little. Think about the moments when you have enough. Don't let social pressure make you buy more, eat more, drink more or order more expensive drinks. In the Dutch version of the book 'Your Money or Your Life' the authors call this 'creative thrift' and 'austerity with style'. Both terms appeal to me. It's about consuming less, it's about consciously and critically looking at whether things can be done differently, with less money and raw materials, more sustainably. It's also about adopting a totally different attitude, only buying something when you need it if you really can't go without it.

I am a great advocate of experimenting. You can try everything out first and because you see it as an experiment you are not psychologically attached to it. You can give yourself more space to experience how you really find something.

A good example of setting up a more ambitious personal experiment is to start with your 'Year of Less'. Take a whole year off to try out, do, evaluate, go through what you like and stop what you don't like. In the book 'The Year of Less' Cait Flanders describes how, with a debt of US$30,000, she challenges herself not to shop and to learn how to feel good again without the distractions of consumerism.

Cait Flanders, The Year of Less: How I Stopped Shopping, Gave Away My Belongings, and Discovered Life is Worth More Than Anything You Can Buy in a Store.

Tip:
Don't do it alone, find a buddy and be sure to discuss it with your partner. Don't keep it to yourself that you are serious, conscious and focused on saving money and growing FYM. Explain what your savings goals and FYM and FIRE goals are. People are more likely to give you space or even help you if they understand what you are doing and what you are doing it for. If necessary, find someone to help you make the right decisions.

The magic of compound interest

This story actually belongs to the next part 'Grow: How do I let my money grow' because it's not about saving money by not spending but about growing money by saving and investing. But because it's so motivating, I'll discuss it here. The essence is: because of the effect of compound interest, saving even small amounts of money over a long period of time causes an enormous growth of your assets. The magic of compound interest shows how you can see money grow. When you earn interest on savings, that interest itself generates interest. The higher the interest or return on investments and the longer the period, the more your money grows!

A calculation: $100 at 5% interest yields $5. The original $100 + $5 interest = $105 at 5% interest yields $5.25 in the next period. If you don't contribute anything for ten years but do receive interest for each period and add it to the principal, that $100 has grown to $160 and the interest you receive that year exceeds €8. If you do contribute for ten years, say at $100 a year, your total amount will grow to around $1300, while you've only deposited $100 ten times = $1,000. This interest-on-interest effect combined with regular deposits for as long as possible can quickly get you close to your FYM and FIRE target.

Why I wanted to introduce this here in this chapter? Because you can also use this magic with the savings on your expenses and deposit your saved money regularly into your savings/investment account.

If you are able to save $25 per week on your groceries and you can save $100 per month, every month, and invest with an average return of 5%, after 10 years there will be more than $15,500 in your account. You have deposited a total of $100 x 120 months = $12,000 and earned $ 3,500 in interest. After 20 years of depositing $100 every month, the interest-on-interest effect is much bigger because of the long duration, you have deposited $24,000 and your balance comes to $41,000, so a return of

$ 17,000. Look again at these numbers: $ 17,000 interest earned from depositing $ 24,000 is more than 70%! That's the magic!

For example, if you are able to save $500 per month, after 10 years you will have about $78,000 and after 20 years more than $200,000.

See the worksheet. You can calculate this yourself with the numbers that are relevant to your situation. You can do this in for example Excel with the function Future Value (FV) and then enter the numbers in the situation above: Interest (interest rate per month) = 4%/12, Number of payments = 120, Payment = $100, PV (your current value, starting balance) = 0)

Or you use a calculator such as:

Money that grows - Magic of Compounding

Compound Interest Calculator

Worksheet with example compound interest at 'Tools'

The message here is twofold:

- Start saving as soon as possible and save as long as possible
- Deposit money regularly

Motivating? First let's see how much you can save then.

Save in 8 steps

As you have come to expect from me by now, I like to bring some structure to things. In order to start saving in a somewhat structured way I distinguish the following steps:

1. Set up your savings system, to keep track of your expenses and analyze savings opportunities and progress.
2. Capture/document your expenses (all expenses!)
3. Analyze your expenses and determine your savings potential.
4. Identify savings opportunities and come up with savings ideas.
5. Budgeting.
6. Pay yourself first, always.
7. Spend less money.
8. Record your progress and adjust where possible.

Steps 1 to 3 in my situation:

I use a Google Sheets document on my phone to document how much I spend on what. Every single purchase! I use a number of categories (nine) and it takes me no effort and very little time. Every once in a while, in the beginning more often than now, I copy all new data on my computer to a total overview of expenses. With this I can start analyzing how I have done and where I see improvement (saving) possibilities or where I want to change my spending pattern and behavior. To see where your money is going on this category level you can either track it directly or if you pay electronically copy the data from your online banking.

This costs me one hour a month. I look at the average daily totals, how they differ during the week, and why. I look at week totals, how they differ during a month, and why. I look at the days with a high average, which categories stand out or differ from what is normal. After a few weeks of tracking, you can try to do a few things differently based on the insights in your spending. You can also start thinking about how much money you actually want to spend on a certain category in a certain period of time.

> **Tip**
> **For step 2 you want to have as much data as possible at your disposal. As you're reading now and maybe don't want to directly go into action mode, I would still advise you to keep track of all your expenses from now on and to keep (a picture of) all receipts of all your purchases. To measure is to know. Soon this will give you insight.**

Step 1: Setting up your savings system, to keep track of your expenses and progress and analyze possibilities.

It sounds a lot more difficult than it is, because you can make your savings system as complicated or simple as you want. And you can adjust and expand your system later, for now ... K.I.S.S. (Keep It Simple Stupid)

I think, the core of such a system consists of:

An Expenses Sheet

An easy to open document on different devices, also useable offline, that automatically syncs between devices. I open this worksheet in Google Sheets on my phone to keep track of my expenses and I open it on my laptop to process the data. I immediately enter the amounts in the appropriate category column. Each category has its own column and every day is a line (row). That's it.

An Expense tracker file

You can also do this in Google Sheets if your Expenses Sheet is set up there but Microsoft Excel or Numbers for Mac also works fine. This file consists of a number of worksheets.

Raw data sheet

A raw data worksheet, in which you load the data from the Expenses Sheet. This can be a copy-paste action, you can also have it done automatically but that's for advanced users and I will stay K.I.S.S. (Keep It Simple Stupid) for now. Each category has its own column and every day is a row.

Data processing worksheet

A data processing worksheet, in which you link to the raw data from the raw data worksheet and in which you add data from your online banking. Each category has its own column and every day is a row. This worksheet has more categories because you also enter the data from your bank statements here.

Groceries worksheet

A Groceries worksheet. This is double work and you probably only use this in the beginning. In my Expenses Sheet, for simplicity's sake, I fill in the different expenses in the categories. In my category groceries of a certain day, all expenses of groceries at different stores at different times are added together and not specified. The groceries worksheet is more detailed with the details of your saved (or photographed) receipts and here you don't use categories but products. With these details you can start looking for savings later on.

Savings worksheet

A savings worksheet is where you later get to work with the data, analyze your expenses and look for savings opportunities.

Expense sheet

Example worksheets with basic admin of expenses

Step 2: Capture your expenses

Capture all your daily expenses in your Expenses Sheet, preferably at the time you spend it, then you're most accurate and don't forget anything. Or at the end of the day based on the totals of your receipts or expenses in online banking. Do this every day. Every dollar, pound or euro.

If you want more insight into where your money is going, you can look at your groceries at product level. For this purpose, you will want to keep or photograph all receipts of your groceries for a month. This sounds awkward and cumbersome but I can't think of any other way. Just do this for one month and use that data.

Complete your data-processing worksheet (at least) once a month with the payments directly (automatically) debited from your account, such as rent/mortgage, gas/water/electricity, mobile/tv/internet subscriptions, etcetera. Please make sure that you do not enter the electronically paid expenses twice.

You can choose (especially in the beginning) to keep it at this, KISS works fine here. You can also choose to further expand this cash book in your spreadsheet and add all kinds of functionalities such as automatically generated overviews and graphs, calculate your Saving Rate etcetera.

You can also supplement your overview with all income. Then you can create a complete cash book with a sum of all individual expenses and revenues for each month. This overview gives you immediate insight into whether you have any money left this month.

There are apps where you can keep track of your expenses (and start budgeting later). Also more and more banks offer features in their online environments to give you more insight into your spending. I will elaborate on this at the end of this chapter.

Step 3: Analyze your expenses and determine your savings potential

Cost drivers categories

You will quickly see, after the first month, if you have any money left and have been able to save money. After the second month you can see if you have been able to save on the things you buy by adjusting your spending behavior and if you have more money left. Looking at this insight quickly becomes addictive, because this is what creating FYM is all about, every dollar or euro you save now counts.

After a few months you will see that there are expensive months and less expensive months, if only because certain things such as annual insurance payments or quarterly leasehold payments will be deducted from your account.

Use this overview to analyze if there are categories where you spend too much money. Now that you have this overview at your disposal, consider whether the amount you spend on your cell phone subscription, or television, or clothing, or eating out is in proportion to what's coming in and what's left at the end.

Take a look at your overview and consider how you would plot all categories in the matrix: easy to save versus difficult to save and little saving potential versus a lot of saving potential.

	Easy to save	Difficulty saving
Little saving potential	***	*
Much saving potential	*****	****

If all goes well, this will give you insight into where you can see low hanging fruit that is easy to pick. The easy to realize savings, preferably with a high savings potential, are the most interesting to start with (5 stars). An example of easy to save and a lot of potential savings is if you regularly use a cab, while you can also cycle or walk. Also, you can already determine what are useful projects that take a bit more time and effort but also yield a lot (4 stars). For example, an expensive contract that can only be cancelled within the terms and conditions without penalty. You have to figure this out and then plan it. The easy to save with little savings potential (3 stars) can also be taken up and implemented. Formulate actions and put them in your action list (app).

What gives me extra insight is to look at percentages from time to time. If you have everything in a spreadsheet, you can easily start playing with the numbers and, for example, calculate the average monthly totals per category for the past 6 months, sort them by size and then calculate them as percentages of the total monthly amount.

Take a look at your overview and classify each category in the matrix: 'large expense item' versus 'small expense item' and 'much personal value' versus 'little personal value'.

	A lot of personal value	Little personal value
Large expense item	***	*****
Low expense item	*	***

By putting some time in this analysis every month you will quickly get a much better feeling about the value of your money and whether or not the things you spend money on are actually worth it. You'll soon find categories or specific expenses that you don't really care about, or that you spend a relatively large amount of money on (5 stars). For many people, the car falls into this category. Is it possible that your a car doesn't really interest you that much and you probably don't use it very much but it does cost a lot of money every month on insurance, maintenance, parking, depreciation? You want this type of expenses to be the first savings success. Even things that don't cost that much money but don't add much value, can easily be stopped.

The most important thing is to put your spending overview next to your dream and goals. Look at the expenditures you've made to see if they were important enough or provided enough value for you when you consider what your dream and goals are and how you've thought about changing your lifestyle. Look at it, capture insights and patterns, come up with new ideas, document and put them in action lists and discuss it with your partner or buddy.

Especially in the beginning you will see that the extent to which you can specify your spending makes a huge difference to what insight you can get out of it. I keep track of the cost of alcoholic beverages in a separate category, whether I buy it in the supermarket or on a terrace or at a restaurant, the fact that I don't include it in the general groceries category makes it clear to me that there really is a lot to save here. I have been able to adjust my behavior and see how much money it saves per month if I fulfill my needs a little differently. Different factors determine my expenses, both the total number of bottles per week, the number of times I buy, the place where I buy (less outside the door). I really enjoy a good glass of wine, I think it's 'important' in that sense and I can continue to enjoy it and still save about 50% on this cost item.

Products cost drivers

You can continue analyzing, if you want to, where your money goes by looking at your groceries. You can look at product level on which you spend money and where there are saving opportunities. An obvious way to save is to buy less of it. But what if you don't want to use less of it? Then you have to buy smarter.

You can find a cheaper alternative for many of the products you buy every day, for example by not buying packaged but loose, by not buying A-brand or name-brand but private label, by buying something not in the supermarket but on the market. In the chapter 'Less bullshit in your life?' I paid quite a lot of attention to the misconception that B-brands or private label products are of inferior quality. Many products come from the same factory. The only difference between an expensive pack of A-brand meadow milk and an ordinary pack of milk from the bottom shelf is the price. The product comes from the same factory, from the same farmer, possibly from the same cow. A well-known secret is that some large FMCG companies produce private label products. Also, many Costco items are actually manufactured under a private label by name-brands just for Costco. Costco has very strict requirements making the product of the same or better quality but they sell it at a fraction of the cost! It's rumored that Starbucks, Pampers, Duracell and even Grey Goose products are sold as Costco private label.

	I buy often	I buy sometimes, almost never
Much savings potential	*****	***
Little savings potential	***	*

A useful insight is to know what things occur on a daily basis and on what you can save a lot but also things that do not occur often and cost a lot of money. So don't be 'Penny wise, Pound foolish', save a few cents on a croissant on the weekend, while choosing to buy expensive takeaway lunch every day.

Add the details of a month's shopping to your Saving worksheet.

- Add a column with the 'Price per item you are paying now.
- Think or search the internet for the price of a cheaper alternative. Add a next column with 'Minimum price' that you can find for another but reasonably similar product, for example a private label instead of a name-brand.
- In the next column 'Price difference per piece' you can calculate the difference between 'Price per piece' and 'Minimum price'.
- In the next column you calculate the 'price difference %', the amount in 'Price difference per piece' divided by the amount in 'Price per piece' (as % or multiplied by 100).
- In the last column you calculate the 'total price difference', this is 'Price difference per piece' times 'Quantity'.
- Add above or below the columns 'Price paid' and 'Price difference' totals, calculate the sum of the total column, you will now see the 'total amount spent' and you will now see the total possible amount to save under 'Price difference total'.
- Calculate the % total savings potential by dividing 'Total price difference' by 'Total amount spent' (as % or multiplied by 100).

What amount can you save in one month by buying smarter? How much is that as a percentage?

- Sort by price difference per piece. On which products do you save the most dollars or euros per piece?
- Sort by price difference %. On which products do you relatively save the most if you buy a cheaper version?
- Sort by quantity. Which product do you buy the most?
- Add up the total price difference for this product (i.e. the price difference x the total quantity per month), how much can you save? Can you buy less of this product?
- Sort by price per piece. Which products are the most expensive?
- Add up the prices for this product, how much does this cost you per month?
- Can you buy less of this product?

Step 4: Identifying savings opportunities and coming up with savings ideas

Books and blogs have been written about consumerism, minimalism, frugality and saving money. Depending on how you feel about it, you'll either find it inspiring or annoying. I would like to try to explain these concepts in a different way and try to mention what I think are the most important principles with which you yourself can come up with ideas for saving in a somewhat structured way. My idea is that there are general principles that you can apply to many different types and categories of cost drivers. Cost drivers to me are everything that you spend money on. Besides your groceries this includes subscriptions, services like insurances and the rent or mortgage of your house.

Where do you spend money on and where can you save?

You can add your own overview of expenses of the past month(s) or you can start with the following list of cost drivers:

- Home
- Water, gas, electricity
- Tax, municipality, garbage collection, ...
- Telephone
- Television
- Internet
- Subscriptions and memberships
- Food
- Drinks
- Transportation
- Eating out
- Going out, out of home drinking, and festivities
- Vacations
- Clothing and shoes
- Home interior, furniture
- Insurances
- Hobbies
- Garden, flowers, plants
- Gifts
- Medical costs
- Services (cleaner, gardener, ...)
- Sports
- Children (can be further specified)
- ...

Large expenses

Before I explain the Smarter, Better, Cheaper principles, let's first have a look at what you ultimately spend the most money on. Chances are that this is also where you can save the most and perhaps the easiest.

It strikes me that with large infrequent expenses we sometimes have very different thoughts and use our rational thinking much less than with small regular expenses. We give freer rein to our emotions. Almost everyone has large incidental expenditures that suddenly do not seem to matter. Examples are vacations, because that's what you've been saving for and deserve. Or a car, because it functions for a long time. Or a wedding, because that's once in a lifetime and no way you're going to save on that. Or a kitchen, because everyone spends so much money on a kitchen. This is the ultimate 'Penny wise, Pound foolish' behavior. You can drink cheaper milk for years, eat no more cookies, only buy private label products and put less sugar in your coffee and then spend it all on a multi-functional steam oven or electric tin opener at once because it fits so nicely in the kitchen wall and the neighbors also have one (and also never use it).

If you look at what you spend in total, the biggest cost drivers are probably your home and if you own one, your car.

Realize that you are going for the long term, for a conscious lifestyle and for money to be saved for the most important things in your life. Think carefully about your lifestyle needs and how to meet them. If you already live in yet another house, which due to lifestyle inflation, has become bigger, nicer and more expensive each time, there is a lot to gain if you are willing to live in a slightly different way or place that better suits your new lifestyle. Can you share your home temporarily, for example when you are on vacation, or permanently, by renting out part of your home, a room, a floor or look for a roommate? Think about how you can make your existing home (more) suitable for this purpose.

Can you move, to a cheaper place or to a smaller house? Geo-arbitrage is a well-known FIRE principle, where you find out what you gain by moving to a cheaper location. This can be a cheaper neighborhood, a bit further away from the center, a state with less (state, local, income) tax or just outside the city.

Car ownership is, in my personal opinion, a kind of a strange phenomenon. For most people and also for myself, owning a car is inseparable from irrational thoughts and emotions. Again, you have to take a good look at your needs and how you fulfill them. Can you do without a car? How much value do you attach to what kind of car you drive? Do you realize how much more, harder and longer you have to work in order to drive an expensive car? Could you maybe look at whether it is enough for you to have a functional car, instead of what society tells you is a good car? There is a huge price difference between a cheap functional car and an expensive luxury car but in the end an expensive car delivers very little 'extra'. Don't buy a new car anyway. Don't lease a car either. Let someone else pay for the enormous depreciation in the first years of a car's life. Buy an easy and inexpensive car to repair with low maintenance costs. Probably for less than $5,000 you can buy a good enough car that meets your functional requirements.

Example: large infrequent cost driver: new kitchen

Kitchen salesmen like to make sure that the total amount you spend is higher than you wanted and ever were planning to spend. This is probably the same in the whole world. They offer you all kinds of extras, often 'for free'. With huge discounts but only if you sign up right away, you get the feeling that it's worth it and that you can't pass up this opportunity. You have to stay strong here and stick to your pre-determined list of requirements, the performances you need and the money you're willing to spend. Google is your friend! Prepare yourself well.

Example: large infrequent cost driver: Wedding

(Hey that sounds so anti-romantic to call a wedding a cost driver...)

For most people, a wedding is a big thing. There are too many people influencing you, there are too many demands you have to meet, there are too many things that are expected from you, there are too many trends, examples, hypes. And it is a business where a lot of money is made. Often unjustified, I think. The costs of the reception venue, the necessary clothing, the food, the drinks, all the prices are raised. As soon as someone knows it's for a wedding, dollar signs appear in the eyes, the red carpet is rolled out and the bottle of bubbly wine appears. Almost everything that is used at a 'standard' wedding is priced way too high. You're most vulnerable when you want something very badly and they know that in this business. It's almost everyone's first time and they know that too. It is, for almost everyone, the only time in their life. People and their parents have been saving all their lives for this special event, and the wedding business knows all that to.

Me and my wife did a lot of things very differently for our wedding. We are still very happy with how we handled it and how it turned out. We organized it ourselves as a project. We did a lot of things ourselves, like arranging the invitations, the decorations but also the bubbly wine, a lot of very good bubbly wine. Of course, our wedding has cost a lot of money, as we really wanted to have a nice festive day with friends. It was very important to us. And it was all worth it!

Don't get carried away, don't give up everything, set a budget and keep your budget under control, make things tiny where possible. Don't outsource everything but do things yourself, it's great fun and saves a lot of money. With creative ideas and by doing a lot of things just a little bit differently, it all works out smarter, better and in the end a lot cheaper.

I'm sure we were able to do everything we wanted for this 'once in a lifetime' event, more even, for a total cost that is at least half of what is spent on average for a comparable wedding. Don't be deterred by the cost and don't let it stop you from organizing a great wedding for yourself, just do it smarter, better and cheaper.

10 Smarter, Better, Cheaper principles

Now that it is clear where savings can be made, ideas can be devised on how to save on the various cost drivers. My idea is that there are general principles that you can apply to all possible types of cost drivers. I list a number of principles that everyone can use to come up with their own savings ideas.

1. Do-it-yourself (DIY)	Learn to do and make things yourself.
2. Segmentation and Skipping	Split something into different parts; use or buy only what you want. Skip steps you don't find interesting or valuable.
3. Turn Lemons into Lemonade	Make the best of something you didn't necessarily want.
4. Kill the contract	The disadvantage of a contract is that you are stuck with it, even if you don't use it. Cancel it or downgrade your contract from premium to freemium (free of charge).
5. Remove the intermediary	Which intermediary earns money off of you and doesn't offer you enough added value?
6. Ownership	Do you really need to own things? Borrow or share with others.
7. Virtualize	Instead of purchasing a physical product or service, we can find a cheaper or often free virtual alternative.
8. Parameter change	Change one or more parameters (variables) and see if you can get the same function out of the product for less money.
9. Geo-arbitrage	Spend money where it's worth the most, buy things where they're cheapest.
10. Image	Stop using image products; you don't have to impress others.

Applying the principles

You can apply the principles yourself to all the above categories on which you spend money and come up with ideas on how to save money.

Step 1: Choose a principle, first write down everything that comes to mind about this principle. What kind of savings ideas can you come up with?

Step 2: Take a look at your overview of expenses for the past month and think about whether you can apply the savings principle, write down all your ideas.

Step 3: Look at your list of ideas and decide which of the ideas you want to try and do next month and which ideas you need to elaborate a bit further, put the ideas in an action list or to do list (app).

Repeat steps 2 and 3 for different categories or products

Repeat from step 1, choose another principle.

Examples Smarter, Better, Cheaper

Geo-arbitrage

Geo-arbitrage is a principle well known to the FIRE community. It is most talked about when it comes to moving to a cheaper location. This is especially relevant if you live in an overpriced neighborhood or city. Search online for the price per square meter or foot of a suitable home in the area where you currently live. Next, look at the square meter or square foot price of a similar home in a less popular area, a little further from the center, outside the city or in another region. Geo-arbitrage to the max is moving to a low-COL country. I talk extensively about Expat FIRE and Nomadic FIRE in 'What shapes and types of FIRE'.

Turn Lemons into Lemonade

We were no longer allowed to rent a scooter during the first lockdown in India. We started to walk everywhere. After being allowed to rent a motorcycle again, we keep walking everywhere because it is much more fun, pleasant and healthier. This saves us money every day. We really didn't need the scooter every day.

Kill the contract

Examples of contracts that are easy to get rid of are newspaper/magazine subscriptions. Buying a newspaper or magazine once in a while when you feel the need is better than throwing a pile of unread newspapers or magazines. Or read articles on the internet and listen to podcasts and see if you still have the need and time for a magazine.

Ownership

There are many ways to share things, so you don't have to buy them, and services that become cheaper per person if you share them. You can share your car with others or use someone else's car through an online platform. You can share tools, you can share all kinds of subscriptions, magazines but also services such as Spotify, Netflix, your cell phone subscription (family). Also think of house and/or pet sitting and house exchange (for vacations).

Virtualize

There are many free podcasts that you can listen to instead of reading articles in magazines, with interviews on serious and less serious topics.

Video conferencing instead of (business) travel and video calls instead of physical visits are good examples of this.

But also use an e-Reader instead of a physical book and borrow digital books from the library. Online shopping gives you access to a wider range of products and more information, as well as better price comparison.

Parameter change

This allows you to look for products where the bullshit factor is high. Change the physical state, gas, liquid or solid. My favorite 'fun' example is using a piece of nice soap instead of luxurious shower gel. Shower gel also contains soap but actually mostly water and some additives. Shower gel is many times more costly than a nice piece of soap.

A lot of meat is frozen or deep chilled after butchering, which makes sense when you consider that it takes 4 to 6 weeks before lamb from New Zealand or Angus beef from Argentina arrives in Europe where it's sold. Beautiful packaging with bullshit cries like 'matured for at least 28 days' is not only there to make you pay extra for this special piece of meat but also to disguise the fact that the meat has been travelling for so long.

Change the concentration or consistency, or time, or frequency. Change the structure or degree of flexibility. Frequency; buy the same product less often, shop less often. The halving principle; halve the quantity you use and see if it still does the job.

Cost per weight (gram/ounce); Compare the final cost per weight of some different brands or packaging.

Another form: coffee made from freshly ground coffee beans is often better and cheaper than Nespresso.

Do-it-yourself

This is a principle that can be applied to many cost drivers: What can you do yourself, where can you leave out the work someone else is doing?

I make my own pizza dough and sauce and will never order pizza again. Making pizza by yourself or with your children is fun, tasty and usually healthier than having a pizza delivered.

Buy vegetables and cut them yourself instead of a pre-cut stir-fry mix, the same with all ready-to-prepare meals, and all the more so with take-out stuff. I actually prepare a much better coffee-to-go myself and it's a lot cheaper.

Fixing your bike, cleaning your house, doing laundry, cycling instead of Uber, designing and organizing your vacations, booking flights, doing workouts.

Segmentation

You can probably split up your mobile phone subscription. If you have a phone with dual sim (I know there is this one brand refusing to offer this feature…) you can buy a cheap data subscription and you can downgrade the subscription for calling.

It is best to buy a mobile phone without a subscription. You will then see the real cost of the device. You then buy a device that you have decided is worth the money. If you buy a device with a subscription, the cost of the device is hidden in the subscription price, which you pay every month for the full duration of the contract.

I bought a smartphone after thinking about what kind of functionalities I need. I made a shortlist of affordable phones and an overview of what they cost online and I bought my phone, which meets all my requirements and wishes, for US$150.

I have been using this phone for two years now, intensively and to my complete satisfaction. The depreciation of this phone, or the monthly cost of the device, is now around US$6 per month. People who buy a top-of-the-range model from one of the more expensive brands pay large amounts of money for it, whether directly at the time of purchase or hidden in the subscription. Many people are paying US$50 per month or more for the phone, without the subscription and without data, with a contract of 24 months.

As described in the book the Latte Factor and as we have seen earlier about the magical effect of compound interest, even a seemingly small saving yields a lot. The difference between paying US$50 per month and US$6 per month for a phone and putting that in a saving or investment account at 5% return during the 24-month contract period will eventually save you US$1,000. If you save this every 24 months, you save US$6,700 of FYM in 10 years and more than US$18,000 in 20 years.

David Bach & John David Mann,
The Latte Factor - Why You Don't Have to Be Rich to Live Rich (2019)

Calculation example Latte factor

Example: your home

Home is probably the largest cost item where you can implement several principles at the same time and save a lot, even though this can be drastic for your lifestyle. Through geo-arbitrage you determine where, in which neighborhood or just outside the city, you get more value for money. You might downsize and live comfortably in a smaller house. You can temporarily rent out or exchange your house.

Example: transport

Also on the large cost item Transport a number of principles can be applied. Most of the time it is a matter of getting rid of the car and cycling/walking where possible. You can share a means of transport where needed (public transport / car / cab). Use the car less often by virtualizing. For functional trips replace the means of transport by a bike but also add a walk more often and experience and enjoy your surroundings.

Step 5: Budgeting

For some people it's enough to keep track of all expenses, to make an overview of them from time to time and to look for insights and ideas to adjust their behavior and spending pattern. For most people it will work (even) better if they start budgeting.

You can go very far in budgeting with detailed budget items for many different categories but for most people a small number of budget categories is enough. The main goal is to avoid running out of money before the month is over. Budgets give extra insight into what you are spending and are an extra motivation to think differently when a budget is running empty.

The most important best practice is to, immediately when money comes into your account, divide it over different budgets and just don't spend more money than is in your budgets. You can draw up your own rules for this. You can transfer money from one budget to another if you feel the need. In any case, you will become more aware of what you are spending and this will help you to further reduce your spending, optimize your spending pattern and keep money for your FYM or FIRE funds.

In a separate section 'Budgeting' I will explain 9 steps budgeting and 50-30-20 budgeting.

Tip:
Make budgeting automatic: plan rent/mortgage, loan repayments and all other regular expenses so they are paid automatically the day after your pay day. Pay yourself first, always, set up automatic transfers to your savings and/or investment accounts. You can use online banking to automatically transfer amounts to different expense accounts after receiving your income.

Step 6: Pay yourself first, always

Whether you budget or not, put money in your savings account as soon as money comes in: pay yourself first, always!

You budget for your piggy bank and don't wait until there probably is no more money at the end of the month. Do this before you do anything else, before you pay bills, go shopping, or spend money in any other way. You can deposit a small amount in the beginning, if you still have little insight into your savings potential and if you think there is little left over. As I described earlier, depositing $100 a month, consistently every month, with an average return of 4% after 10 years yields more than $14,800, while you probably won't miss the money you first paid yourself at all.

It remains important to be practical and it is not advisable to go negative with your bank account or use your credit card or take on debt in any other way because you run out of money at the end of the month. Make sure that the money you have in your savings account is available immediately and free of charge. This is not money you invest.

Tip:
I mentioned this earlier and I will advise it again later: Make it a habit after a salary increase to add (a large part of) the extra net amount that comes into your account directly to your savings account. After all, you don't suddenly have to change your lifestyle and spending pattern and make extra expenses now that you're making more money. This prevents lifestyle inflation.

Step 7: Spend less money

The problem is that you don't necessarily have control about how you can earn more. What you do have control over is spending less'.
Patrick Rhone, author of the book 'enough

Now that you have arrived at this step it is time to put into practice what you have come up with in terms of ideas and behavioral changes. I suggest that you immediately start with the easiest things and experiment with what seems more difficult.

- Keep reminding yourself what you're doing it for, as thought up in 'What do YOU want' and 'What are your dreams? Moonshot'!
- Get into the habit of deciding about everything if you think it's worth it. Choose not to do it or buy it if you think it's too expensive for what you get.
- Think if something is a habit and just easy, or if you find it important.
- Keep track of your expenses and regularly monitor the development of your Burn-Rate, your average spending per day.

Patrick Rhone,
enough (2016)

Is 'just good' good enough?

If you're used to only being satisfied with the best of everything, it will come as no surprise to you that you choose the most expensive option by default, of everything, every time. Try the Smarter, Better, Cheaper perspective as you look at the products you always choose. Try looking for best value for money instead of best performance or best tested. You don't choose an inferior product with either, but with the best value you choose Smarter, Better, Cheaper.

Examples of basically just spending less money

Finally, I would like to give a few examples of the effect of simply spending less money, without getting the feeling that you can't live or enjoy yourself anymore. I use the magic of compound interest and the same calculation as before to achieve a total saving, with an average return of 5%.

Two examples:

- Making your own food or drink to go will save you an unlikely amount of money (DIY).
- Getting used to looking for cheaper options when entering into a long-term commitment immediately results in cost savings that last as long as you use them.

And what does that yield?

- Bring DIY lunch with you. No more expensive lunch, take-out or company restaurant. Save 4 x per week $7,50. This is after 10 years about $18,600 on your FYM account.
- DIY coffee. No more trendy expensive coffee in instagrammable cups. Save 5 x a week $5 and save more than $15,000 in 10 years.
- Take advantage of discounts and special offers and buy private labels more often. Save $50 per week in the supermarket. In 10 years this will yield more than $31,000.
- Save on monthly costs of mobile phone, internet, Spotify and ditch your television/cable subscription. For example, if you save a total of $50 per month (and depending on your situation there's a lot more to be achieved here) you'll save almost $8,000 in 10 years.
- Negotiate a better energy deal, with your current energy supplier or with the competitor. Save $35 per month, save more than $5,400 in ten years.

I'm not talking at all about more difficult choices such as the big expenses for your house, a car or a big vacation or wedding. If you only apply the above minimal lifestyle adjustments, you will save almost US$80,000 in ten years! That's Fuck You Money! You can make dreams come true, do things that matter to you. Do the same for 20 years and you'll have a nice start to a FIRE sum of over US$200,000 only because of a few smart choices.

Sample calculation
Just spend less

Step 8: Record your progress and adjust where possible

I discussed the importance of recording your expenses and receivables earlier. As a last step of Saving, you want to measure your progress, do reviews and adjust your way of working where possible and necessary.

Keep your progress next to your ambitions. Celebrate successes and milestones. Think about if this works for you, how well it works, and if you want to approach something differently. Determine actions and record them in action lists or To Do-apps. Check if you can tick off actions or are postponing them.

Do reviews, with your partner or find a buddy if you don't have a partner.

Budgeting

"A budget is telling your money where to go instead of wondering where it went."

Dave Ramsey an American presenter, author and businessman.

Budgeting in 9 steps

Setting up your budgets is easiest when you have a few months to a year of data on what you have spent. Optimizing your budgets can be done on a monthly basis. Once you have mastered the budgeting, make sure that every dollar, pound or euro is used the way you want it.

You can look up your payment details by scrolling through your online banking, adding or estimating your credits and debits and by totaling per category. You can probably also download this in a file, you'll need to edit it to make it useful for you. Fortunately, this is a one-time job.

Step 1: Determine your total monthly net income, including everything.

Add up all your non monthly income from last year (vacation pay, bonus, ...), divide it by 12 and add it to your total monthly net income.

Step 2: Make a list of Necessary expenses categories.

Necessary expenses are the expenses you have to pay each month and which are essential for your housing, work or other obligations. These are needs, must haves.

Step 3: Make a list of categories Personal Choices.

Personal choices are expenses that you invariably make and spend on the things you can do without but that you choose to spend money on. These are wants, optional.

Step 4: Estimate the cost.

Once you have named all your spending categories you can assign monetary values to them, month by month per category, based on averages of past months or years.

Step 5: Calculate the value of your monthly 'Savings'.

Once you have budgeted your monthly total net income and determined an initial budget for all spending categories, you can see how much is left to save from these expenses and revenues.

Step 6: Assign spending limits

'Pay yourself first, always' elaborates on the rule that you first give yourself a budget to save instead of saving what you end up with at the end of the month.

In 'The 50/30/20 budget' I explain how to make a start with spending limits for the main categories. Start budgeting your monthly Savings by calculating 20% of your total net monthly income. Then budget Necessary expenses. Add these values up and subtract them from your total net monthly income and you have your budget for Personal Choices. If you are in debt, you can charge your loan payments to Savings but you can also include a separate item within Necessary expenses.

Step 7: Search for saving opportunities.

Your goal is to increase the Savings budget. Earlier you explored your saving potential and saving possibilities. Think about the effect on your budgets Necessary expenses and Personal choices and lower the spending limits so that your Savings budget becomes higher.

Step 8: Pay yourself first, always. Spend less money. Keep track of your expenses.

Once you've set your spending limits for the month, track your spending and keep track of when you reach a limit in each category. When you reach your limit, you stop spending money in that category.

If you spend more in one category than budgeted, you can see if you can get money from another budget category. Then you stay within your total monthly budget and don't touch your savings budget.

Step 9: Look back and look ahead.

After you've completed your first month of budgeting, you'll see how you've spent. This is a good time to determine which categories you can reduce your budget and you can make adjustments for categories in which you have spent more than you planned for and where you expect to spend it in the future.

This is the time to think about which budget category you want this budget increase to be charged to, in other words, which categories you can reduce by the same amount. You want to avoid this as much as possible at the expense of Saving.

Please make sure that you have budget items for major expenses that are coming up, such as insurance premiums or leasehold or rents that are only due every few months. It's up to you whether you include certain budget items in Savings such as a vacation budget or whether you include them in Personal Choices and really keep your Savings for more than a year. In 'Paying and Saving money' I discuss different types of savings accounts and the necessity and possibilities of an emergency fund.

The first two or three months of budgeting are the hardest because you may need to adjust your budget items, limits and categories a few more times while at the same time you are already working on reducing your expenses.

You can use the categories you defined in step 4 of 'Save in 8 steps' but it is also possible that this is too detailed for your budgets, in which case you can then merge a number of categories. You might want to combine House, Gas, Water, Electricity, Internet, home insurance, etc. for budgeting purposes into one budget item Housing. To save money you will of course keep looking at the details.

The 50/30/20 budget

It's not by accident that I let you divide your budget into three parts: Necessary Expenses, Personal Choices and Savings. This is because I want to introduce you to the 50/30/20 budget. This can help you determine your budgets.

This wisdom comes from Elizabeth Warren, a former professor at Harvard. She invented the 50-30-20 rule for budgeting and wrote a book about it in 2005. In addition to the steps described above, Warren recommends that you organize your budget as follows.

The 50/30/20 budget indicates how much you can spend on the different main categories. Twenty percent should be available for 'Savings'. This is essential because, if you have paid yourself first, you can make up the rest.

Fifty percent of your net income can be spent on 'Necessary expenses'. This represents all essential items in your budget such as housing, utilities, transportation, parking fees, insurance premiums and groceries. It also includes things like childcare. However, the fact that these expenses are essential does not mean that we cannot reduce them.

You could say that everything else is not necessary, but this is where the lines begin to blur. The reality is that we make many of our purchasing decisions subjectively rather than objectively. Thirty percent of your net income can be spent on your Personal Choices or Wants. This 30% includes non-essential things, things you do spend money on but can also live without (although life might get a bit sparse). This includes things like eating out, leisure activities, hobbies and personal care.

It can be motivating to call this your 'Fun Stuff' budget. This is where you pay for the fun stuff from. Working with a Fun Stuff budget makes you aware that this is not an endless source and that you will have to make choices here. But within this category you can alternate. One month you spend money on one thing and the next on something else fun. From this budget you can also fill in your personal need for bullshit stuff. Things you don't buy if you don't have the money but if you don't run out of budget, you can spoil yourself.

It can still be difficult to distinguish between 'Necessary Expenses' and 'Personal Choices'. The essential need for a place to live does not mean that you have to live in a palace. Clothing is essential and necessary in itself but not necessarily those new sneakers.

The first thing you get from applying this method is that if you look at your current data for the past months or rather the whole year, you can immediately see where your problems are if you are not in balance. Adjust your lifestyle and spending pattern so that your spending doesn't exceed 50/30/20 budgets.

Do you spend more or less than 50% of your disposable income on what you call Necessary Expenses? Will you make it with 30% of your disposable income for all your Personal Choices'?

If budgeting this way doesn't help you, don't pay too much attention to it. Avoid losing yourself in the details.

Elizabeth Warren,
All Your Worth: The Ultimate Lifetime Money Plan (2005)

Don't budget and still don't overspend

You may have reasons for not wanting to budget. For example, you may find it irritating or unnecessarily complicated. To avoid having nothing left at the end of the month, I will share an alternative method.

This method builds on previously discussed 'rules' but does not require the calculation and tracking of budgets. You can make up your money every month if you make sure that the most important things have been paid first. It becomes more of a guideline on how to spend your money, rather than a list of rules that limit your spending. It may sound and feel better to talk about spending money instead of not spending it.

Having money to spend without budgeting:

- Pay yourself first, always. Immediately after receiving your income, deposit money into your savings account(s) and investment account.
- Then first pay all your bills (these are your 'necessary expenses'), preferably fully automatic and preferably as soon as possible after receipt of income.
- Reserve any money in a (savings) account separate from your spending account for items you expect to have to pay in the future.
- All the money you now have left in your spending account can be spent. This is your 'Fun Stuff' money. Spend it until it's gone.

In real life it works as follows for me (from this you can deduce that I don't budget):

Money arrives in two different private accounts for me and my wife. Immediately a part is transferred to a joint account.

From the joint account, all bills are paid (automatically as much as possible). This account is emptied every month. If anything remains, it can be transferred to the joint savings account.

The joint account includes a savings account from which large, planned and unplanned expenses can be paid. Immediately a part is transferred to a FYM savings account, this is also the place for our emergency fund. From this savings account money can be transferred to the investment account. We don't touch this money.

Immediately a part is transferred to a Personal Choices payment account. From this account small expenses are made, cash money is withdrawn, etcetera. If this account becomes empty (every month) it is a sign that our money is gone and we have to make choices.

I keep track of all expenditures and that gives me sufficient insight at the moment I want to see if I can save more.

FIRE Saving Rate

With a 50/30/20 budget you can save for necessary and beautiful things in the future. But for many people saving 20% of their income is not enough to reach their FYM or FIRE goals. The 20% is a great starting point but probably not the end.

Your Saving Rate (SR) is an important indicator for yourself and is also widely discussed and shared by many in the FIRE community. The SR is the total amount saved as a percentage of your total net income, calculated retrospectively. The goal of most people who save for FYM and FIRE is to increase their SR a little every year.

In addition, you can choose to increase your SR significantly if you are going to earn more, for example after a salary increase or promotion. Instead of spending more money after a salary increase, you start saving more money. The result every month is more money added to your savings account and a higher SR. This is one of the easiest ways to save more money for investing. You don't have to save on anything for this. It prevents lifestyle inflation. You stay satisfied with how everything is and you don't require, now that you have more income, a lifestyle upgrade, which you will quickly get used to again and which quickly becomes the new norm. I think it makes sense, for example, to add 50% to 75% of your net salary increase to your monthly savings and use only 25% to 50% of your salary increase to compensate for real inflation and for the things in life that cost a little more money as you get older.

The SR is important for FIRE because, no matter how much money you earn, a higher SR will bring you to FI faster. It is correct that the absolute amount you save determines how much your FIRE pot grows. It is more important to understand that it depends very much on the disposable income you need to make your desired living how soon you will achieve FI. If you can make a monthly living of US$1,500, you are more likely to become FI sooner than if you need US$4,500 a month.

An example calculation to explain this. In all three cases, US$2,000 per month is saved, which is a considerable amount. The FIRE target number is calculated using the 4% or 25x rule: disposable income x 12 months x 25. The number of years of saving

I calculate in Excel with the Nper (number of periods) function, with a monthly deposit of US$2000, 4%/12 return per month, and the FIRE target that differs per situation.

	Situation 1	Situation 2	Situation 3
Net income	$10,000	$4,000	$3,000
To spend on lifestyle	$8,000	$2,000	$1,000
Savings per month	$2,000	$2,000	$2,000
Saving Rate	20%	50%	67%
FIRE target amount	$2,400,000	$600,000	$300,000
Save Months (Nper)	484	208	122
Number of years saving	40	17	10
You put in a total of	$967,271	$416,581	$243,684
Interest	4%	4%	4%

Situation 1: The disposable income is US$10K, you save US$2K, your SR is 0.2 or 20%. You need a FIRE target amount of US$2,400,000. You need to save 40 years to become FI if you need US$8,000 per month to pay your bills.

Situation 2: Your disposable income is US$4K, you save US$2K, your SR is 0.5 or 50%. Your FIRE target amount here is US$600,000. If you save US$2,000 a month and you need US$2,000 a month to live on, it will take you 17 years.

Situation 3: Your disposable income isUS$3K, you manage to save a lot, again US$2,000, your SR here is 0.67 or 67%. Your FIRE target amount is US$300K. In the end you only spend $1,000 on your lifestyle, you are FI much sooner, after 10 years only.

My point with these examples is that your SR and the amount of disposable income you think you will need to pay for your cost of living after your FI moment, determine how easy or how difficult it will be to reach your FI goal.

3 Saving Rate example calculation

Help with saving and budgeting with apps and online banking

There is software and there are apps you can use to make the budgeting process easier. Banks are also coming up with new features online and in apps to get a better handle on your spending. Take a look at what's possible at your bank.

Budgeting apps

Quicken is perhaps the best-known budgeting software but relative newcomers such as Mint, Mvelopes and You Need a Budget (YNAB) also have many fans. Budgeting apps such as You Need a Budget (YNAB) make it very easy to assign categories, adjust the amounts and keep track of your expenses but it costs money to use the app, which you then can't save. Rates for each of these services vary significantly, so compare features and costs to decide which one is best for you, if you decide you want to pay for such an app. You can also check them out and be inspired by the way of working and the overarching principles before you start paying to use the app.

Good old spreadsheets

You can very well build your own system in which you only use the functions you deem necessary. If you are familiar with Excel, Numbers or Google Sheets, you can very well create your own spreadsheet. You can download or copy bank and credit card data, automated or not, into your spreadsheet to fill in amounts and categories of income and expenses. Personally, I think it gives me extra insight to occasionally copy my manually entered data to my spreadsheet. This is one of the moments for me to get another feel for what I have spent. And the simplicity of my own Google Sheet to keep track of my expenses, with one line per day and columns for each category still ensures that I personally don't use an app for this.

Tip:
There are online courses (e.g. via Coursera) and books to borrow or buy about Microsoft Excel for beginners. Advanced users can take a look at Excel/VBA to further expand and automate your system.

 Microsoft Excel 2019 for Dummies, Greg Harvey

 Microsoft Excel VBA for Dummies, Michael Alexander

Chapter 13
Grow: How do I grow my money

Paying and saving money

Bank accounts (or more accurately current accounts (UK) or checking accounts (US)) are designed to process transactions, such as paying bills or withdrawing cash you need for daily expenses, and nothing else. Being a zero-interest account the amount on your checking account should be only sufficient to pay your monthly bills and withdraw cash for other expenses without you going into overdraft. It is not necessary to keep a very large buffer on your checking account because this can tempt you to spend too much.

To make a good estimation of how much money you want to keep in your checking account you can see how much money you have spent in the past months. You decide how much you want to save and you estimate how much you will have left to spend on personal expenses (wants) after you have made the necessary expenses (needs).

If you assume that you can pay all the normal expenses from your checking account, you can deposit everything that is left at the end of the month into your savings account.

Different kinds of savings accounts

You can now think of which savings accounts you need. You can reserve a part of the money you save for. You don't want to tie up this money, you want to be able to withdraw it immediately and without penalty. You don't want to invest it at a high risk because you have to be able to count on it being available.

You can also reserve part of the money you save for real emergencies, such as redundancy, which we call your personal emergency fund. You can also set other goals for yourself and reserve parts of your savings for this purpose. You probably want to set aside part of your savings for the long term and see how you can make it grow. You may also want to save for retirement, this can be tax advantageous if you do this in a special pension account.

With some online banks you can set up savings goals and open a virtual savings account per savings goal. At other banks you can open extra accounts easily and free of charge. Find out what the possibilities are at your bank. You can also, if you have a partner, open a joint account and deposit money here with your partner, which will make it your total budget for all joint monthly expenses.

If you do have a joint account, you can also open a joint savings account and dedicate it specifically to the savings purposes 1 to 3 below.

In addition, you will probably open an investment account with one or more financial service providers. Not every savings account is necessarily a separate savings account. This way you can easily put part of the money from several savings accounts into one savings account or even invest it and for that you do not necessarily have to open a separate account every time. Find out what works for you and then set it up.

I distinguish 6 different savings accounts:

1. General savings account for unplanned necessary expenses.

This is a savings account, not for investing. It's your budget for things like replacing your washing machine or repairing your house (e.g. after a leak), maintenance of your car, etcetera. You know this is likely to happen once in a while, and you can put in some money every month so that you can easily pay these kinds of necessary expenses. You can easily look back on the past years and make an estimate of your required budget per year. For most people this will be a few hundred to a few thousand dollars, pounds or euros, depending on whether you rent or own your house and whether you have a car, for example.

2. Saving for planned large expenses.

This can be part of your general savings account. It's more of a budgeting action to keep a separate pot for things you plan to do or buy. It is nice to put some money in this account every month for major maintenance of your house, such as a five-yearly outdoor painting job. Also, for example, a vacation budget to which you deposit some money every month and to which you can also put your vacation money you might receive. Replacing your car if necessary is also something you can plan and budget for. This kind of occasional expenses will cost you a small monthly amount instead of a huge unexpected sum if you have not thought about this. Now you don't have to think about it anymore, you can plan your vacation or arrange for your maintenance, even when your checking account doesn't seem to allow it. Again, this money you will not invest, it is at a low interest rate on a savings account.

3. Personal Emergency Fund.

You want to prevent any incident from having a major effect on your income that could lead to personal bankruptcy. You don't want to get stressed out because you think you can not pay your bills. Especially if you are self-employed, you want to make sure that you can continue to live without any income for at least a few months to a few years. If you are an employee, you want to be able to supplement your income from benefits, for example, when you are laid off by your employer, so that you can pay all your bills and look for a new job without stress for at least a few months to six months. An unforeseen event such as a financial, economic or health crisis can have a high or low impact depending on your situation. Your personal emergency fund gives you breathing room, no matter what happens.

4. Fuck You Money (FYM).

So that in the future you have the freedom to make your own choices that are important to you. Depending on your timeline, you can invest (part of) your FYM, hoping that your return will be higher than you can expect with a savings account. By definition, you run a higher risk of not getting the return you want, so you need to assess how flexible you can be at the moment you want to use your FYM.

Both the target number of your FYM amount and your Grow strategy, the way of growing your money, are to a greater or lesser extent determined by how specifically you can determine what you want to be able to do from your FYM and what your timeline is. When do you want to use FYM, how long will it take, what are you going to do and what will it cost you?

Years ago, I worked towards a FYM amount of $30K after which I resigned from my corporate job. Then I used $17.5K for travelling the world for a year. After that I spent the remaining money from my FYM account to start my own business.

From the moment I started to make money again and I had money left over, I replenished my FYM account to about $95K after which (ten years later) I left on a trip with my wife for an indefinite time. The largest part of this trip cost on average about $2,600 per month (for two persons, including everything). Three years of travelling has cost me about $95K.

5. FIRE fund

So that you have the choice to quit paid work and retire early.

6. Private supplementary pension.

This can be very specific to the country you live in. In general, it's safe to say it can be interesting to invest money in some kind of private supplementary pension because there are tax advantages to be gained here. Depending on your situation it can be necessary if, for example, you do not accrue a full pension, or if your pension commences earlier, or if a pension is not provided for you anyway. For the self-employed it can be even more important to build up a comfortable pension capital for later.

About that emergency fund

Do I really need an emergency fund? Yes, you do!

Most people choose to put this emergency fund in a savings account, at low interest rates, and not invest it. You want your emergency fund to be available and you want to run as little risk as possible. Especially in a crisis situation you don't want to sell funds or be confronted with a diminished value of your portfolio. You want to be able to withdraw this money immediately and without penalty 'when the shit hits the fan'.

The amount of your emergency fund depends on your situation but that you need an emergency fund is beyond any doubt. This is for real emergencies and here you have to think worst-case scenario, expect the unexpected, assuming that even the most unexpected can happen so you need cash. Bankruptcy, redundancy, an accident resulting in disability or a severe form of illness such as cancer can have enormous financial consequences, both on the income and expense side. Assume the stock market crashes, for such a situation you need an emergency fund.

How much do you need? Everyone has a different opinion. Most 'experts' suggest that you have at least enough for six months of spending: if you need US$3,000 of your disposable income to survive each month, make sure you have an emergency fund of US$18,000 in case you can't expect any income in case of an emergency.

Most people (in Europe) who have a reasonably stable employer, such as the government or in a well-organized industry, need around $6 to $10K.

If you are self-employed, you should take a good look at your monthly cost of living. Depending on your lifestyle, age, (in)security of your industry, flexibility, risk aversion, etcetera, you want to build up emergency funds for at least six months to a few years.

Does that fund really have to be in the savings account? The interest rate is extremely low but you want to feel really safe, make sure you have backup, withdraw it immediately. Depending on your situation, you decide what is wise but if you come up with a worst-case scenario in which you want to count on your emergency fund at the moment of a stock market crash, you understand my point.

About repaying your debt first

As long as your debts are greater than your possessions and assets, on balance you don't own anything at all, and you are not on your way to FI. As long as the costs of your debts (the interest to be paid) are greater than the proceeds of your assets (the interest to be received), your financial situation deteriorates, and you run the risk of never even getting out of debt.

If you have a student loan or student debt and you want to buy a house this generally has negative consequences, it is more difficult to get a mortgage or the amount you can borrow is lower.

The message is clear, pay off your debts. Having said that, currently (2020) there is an extraordinary situation with extremely low interest rates. This rare situation enables a so-called leverage effect, where you are able to borrow money at low cost and you can invest this money at a higher yield. According to economic theories, this situation cannot exist for a long time. You run the risk of not being able to repay your debt when your investments returns are disappointing.

Without going into too much detail, I personally think it is wise to pay off your debts as soon as you can, while in some situations you simultaneously can start investing. You want to start paying off those debts where the costs are high in order to reduce your debt burden, whilst at the same time reducing your monthly (fixed) costs. In the meantime, it is also interesting to see if you can refinance and reduce the cost of your loans, by lowering the interest rate, if you still suffer from high interest rates.

You should treat debts with really high interest rates, such as personal loans and credit card debt, as emergencies and paying them off should be your priority before you even start saving or investing.

Relatively small debts or debts with low interest costs are less urgent. But realize that in the end you want to get rid of them in time.

Saving, investing

You save the money you don't use to live and pay the bills and this money you want to grow. There are roughly three ways to make your money grow:

1. You can put it on a savings account and receive interest on it.
2. You can invest in equities like stocks in the hope of receiving dividends and increasing the value of your investments.
3. You can invest in a company or real estate.

Money in a savings account

Savings accounts are currently (2020) not interesting to grow your assets due to the incredibly low interest rates. The most important reason to put your money in a savings account is risk reduction and diversification. You can park money you need in the short or medium term in a savings account.

There is an alternative to the regular savings account. You can put your savings in deposits, which means that you park your money for a longer period of time and cannot withdraw it immediately without paying a fine. You can choose to deposit your money for a period of 3, 6 or 9 months, one, two or five years. The longer you deposit your money, the more interest you get. At the moment (2020) the interest rate for deposits is too low for me to be a serious alternative.

Invest in stock market

You want a high return but not too much risk. The most important thing is to find the balance between risk and return expectation which you feel comfortable with. Simply put, you can put your money in different types of investments, and it is up to you to determine which part of your assets you put in which type of investment.

You can adapt your strategy to your (life)phase and the time you have left to reach your goal. In the beginning you can choose a more aggressive strategy, with a higher risk profile and a higher expected return. As time goes on, you can become more defensive, because you don't want to run the risk of having to get out during a crash at the very moment you want to travel or stop working.

The most important basic principles in investing are:

- Minimize investment costs
- Spread investments
- Invest for the long term
- Know what not to invest in
- Avoid investments you don't understand

Check every investment opportunity that you're considering on these five principles. In this chapter I want to explain only what's relevant for you in growing your money to achieve your FYM and FIRE goals. I actually think that most of the information about investing in individual stocks, bonds, commodities and currencies is not very relevant, interesting or important to the average FYM and FIRE investor. You probably don't want to become an investor anyway. However, I will try to explain briefly what investing is about so that you can better understand what we are talking about when we speak of investing in, for example, an ETF that tracks an index of shares in companies that operate globally.

I suggest you find a website of a relevant shareholder association in your country. I know for example this exists in the UK (UKSA), the Netherlands (VEB), Australia (ASA), New Zealand (NZSA) and Sweden (Aktiespararna). In the US a trustworthy source of information is www.investor.gov by the US Securities and Exchange Commission. This could be a good starting point for some more information and knowledge about investing in your country because they are independent of banks, brokers, investment funds and advisors.

The main relevant categories of investments are:

Shares/Stocks	Options & Futures
Bonds	Investment funds
Real estate	Indextrackers
Commodities	ETFs
Currencies & Crypto currencies	

A large part of my capital is invested in my own real estate. I currently gain passive income from it and it's increasing in value, that's my expectation. This is, besides my savings account, the low-risk part of my investments. Therefore, I don't think I need to invest in bonds or real estate funds.

I also bought a number of individual shares at the time I thought it was right (market timing) and I will keep these in the coming years (buy and hold).

In addition, I have a portfolio of widely diversified index ETFs with different regional focuses.

Shares

The first thing most people think about when it comes to investing is the stock market. The images of traders can appeal to the imagination and you can almost see (feel) that it's about making (and losing) money.

Shareholders own shares of a company. Most shareholders have no direct control over a company's activities and that is not what most shareholders are concerned with.

It is very easy to buy shares, either through your bank's investment account or through a separate investment account at a specialized financial institution, the broker.

Supply and demand determine the level of the share price. The bid price is the maximum price at which the buyer with the highest bid wants to buy. The ask price is the minimum price at which a seller wants to sell the same share. In principle, you buy at your bid price and sell at your offer price. Stock trading is often very liquid, i.e. transactions usually take place quickly.

There are different types of orders. The most common are market orders, limit orders and stop orders. A market order buys (or sells) shares at the prevailing market prices until the order is executed. This is also called an at-best order. No price limit is given. A limit order specifies a certain price at which the order must be executed, although there is no guarantee that part or all of the order will be traded if the limit is set too high or too low. A stop order is a type of limit order, which is triggered when a stock moves above or below a certain level. Stop orders are often used as a way to limit larger losses (or to fix profits) and are therefore also called stop-loss orders.

You sell shares in much the same way as you buy shares. Place an order to sell online and wait for the order to be executed when a buyer is found. If you can't sell, you're asking too high a price at that time. You can lower your price or wait.

Trading and making money by buying and selling shares is very simple: you buy for a low price and sell for a high price.

And this also makes it immediately clear how easy it is to lose money. If you don't sell at the right time or if you clearly buy at the wrong time, you make a loss.

Bonds

A bond is a fixed-interest financial instrument that represents a loan from an investor to a borrower, just like an IOU (I owe you), a (written) promise to pay back a debt. Bonds are used by companies, municipalities and governments to finance projects and their budget (of the country).

I think everyone agrees that bonds are the least sexy part of your investment portfolio, but they can be important because they normally provide the best protection against deflation. The fixed interest rate becomes worth more in the event of a general decline in prices. At the moment the interest rate is very low, and it cannot be ruled out that the interest rate will rise and that bonds will become worth less. That is why bonds are now even less popular than usual.

If you have a long-term horizon and invest well spread (through ETFs) and count on fluctuations, dips and crashes to eventually pay off, I see no reason to invest in bonds to achieve your FYM and FIRE goals. If you wish, ETFs are available in global bonds.

Options and Futures

I address options and futures only because everyone who has ever thought about investing has probably heard about options and futures. Also, options and futures are regular topics in the news, e.g. because of option schemes of directors and executive board members. It should become clear that options and futures are too complex and risky for most FIRE investors.

If you want to invest in options or futures, it is advisable to study this in depth. The only advantage I can come up with is that you use options or futures to reduce risks but if you already limit your risks with good diversification this is not really necessary.

A share option gives the buyer the right but not the obligation, to buy (or sell) a share at a specified price at any time during the term of the contract. It is like taking a paid option on a hotel room or an option on the purchase of a house. You can take options on stocks, bonds, currencies and stock indices as well as on precious metals and commodities such as orange juice. Options have a leverage effect and are focused on the short term. You can make a lot of money quickly with options but also lose a lot.

A futures contract gives the buyer the obligation to buy a specific product or financial instrument and gives the seller the obligation to sell and deliver the same at a specific future date, unless the holder's position is closed before the expiration date. This is also the reason why a negative futures price on crude oil was possible not so long ago. The holders of the barrels of oil could not get rid of the oil, the tanks were full, so you would get money if you could have and hold the oil at a time in the near future. Futures work with leverage which greatly increases the nominal value of your position. You understand that the future is more suitable for the larger and/or more experienced investor.

Currencies

You can easily buy foreign currency in the hope of exchange rate gains. Exchange rates are extremely volatile and investing in currencies is, in my opinion, more suitable for gamblers than for investors.

You can also use buying currencies to mitigate currency risk (hedging). By doing so, you want to prevent fluctuations in exchange rates from having an effect on the price of shares and ETFs.

Hedging currency risks for equities is complex, costly and risky. As far as I'm concerned, it's better to hold as many of your investments in your own currency as possible and see how the global spread of your investments combined with ETFs does not make you too dependent on a particular region or country. There are also hedged variants of some investment funds, where low costs are charged for hedging currency risks.

Cryptocurrencies

Cryptocurrencies are an alternative investment option. Bitcoin is the best known. So-called cryptos are an emerging technology with a high risk and possibly a high return. Bitcoin has experienced huge value increases but also lost about three quarters of its value in 2018. For me personally, this falls very clearly into the category: Avoid investments you don't understand and this probably applies to most FIRE investors.

Mutual funds

Investment funds or mutual funds are designed to relieve you, the investor, of some of the worries and complexity involved in investing and to allow you to take advantage of opportunities that are available on the market but that are difficult or impossible to organize yourself.

Mutual funds are companies that bundle the money of a group of investors and invest it in various securities, such as shares and bonds. As an investor you buy a share in the mutual fund. Mutual funds have different investment objectives, to which their portfolios are geared to and for which you can choose. The fund managers are responsible for the fund and generate income for investors by making purchases and sales within the fund.

Mutual funds offer you a way to diversify your position. You can put a relatively small amount of money into one or more funds and invest it in 20 to 30 different securities. Many investment funds offer you the opportunity to buy in a specific industry or region or to buy shares with a specific growth strategy.

Here is a number of possibilities:

- Sector funds invest in companies within a specific industry or sector of the economy.
- Growth funds focus on capital growth through a diversified portfolio of companies that have shown above-average growth.
- Value funds invest in companies that are undervalued.
- With index funds, investors can follow the entire market by putting together a portfolio that attempts to match or track a market index. More about this later.
- Bond funds generate monthly income by investing in government and corporate bonds and other debt instruments.

To run a mutual fund involves costs which will be passed along to investors by charging fees and expenses. The fees charged by different funds can vary a lot and have a big impact on your return.

A disadvantage of an actively managed fund, according to many investors, is that the brokers are paid when they make transactions and thus they benefit from making many transactions. The cost of managing the investment fund is the biggest dealbreaker.

Index funds

An index fund is a type of investment fund or mutual fund that strives to track the performance of a market index like the S&P 500 Index.

A market index measures the performance of a 'basket' of securities (such as stocks or bonds) intended to represent a sector of a stock market or an economy. You cannot invest directly in a market index but because index funds follow a market index, they offer an indirect investment option.

Because index funds are generally managed passively, they may be able to save costs. Index fund managers don't have to select securities because they follow the index. Not all index funds have lower costs than actively managed funds. Always make sure you understand the true costs of a fund before investing.

Why FIRE investors are no fans of investment advisors

In short: because your interest is not their interest. Or in other words: if someone knows the golden rules to achieve high returns, why does that person even work in an office?

When thinking about using a financial advisor please think about 'How does he earn his money?' and 'Does he invest in what he advises?'.

Financial advisors earn their salaries mainly on the basis of bonuses when they bring in a new client and on fees, like commission, on what clients buy and therefore not on the basis of the client's return on investment. There are also situations where an hourly rate is charged and charging a percentage of assets under management is normal.

Advisors but also fund managers earn from your transactions, not from your returns. They don't even really benefit from limiting your risk. It is highly unlikely that your adviser or fund manager will be able to beat the index. And remember, if it seems too good to be true, it probably will be.

To invest in an index you simply don't need an advisor or manager. So you can save costs, commissions and percentages!

Why do many people lose money in the stock market?

'Greed is good' is a well-known statement by Gordon Gekko in the movie Wall Street. But for most investors, the innate human tendency to greed is a big risk. We buy when a stock is going well (and it may be overpriced) and we don't want to sell our stock when we should (because we hope it gets better). There exist at least 99 thinking errors, or systematic deviations from logic, and from optimal, rational, reasonable thinking and behavior. See again the book 'The Art of Thinking Clearly' by Rolf Dobelli.

A warning from FIRE investors to other FIRE investors:

- You can't time the market (market-timing).
- You cannot choose a winning stock (stock-picking). Anyone can be lucky but if you really believe in luck you can also go to the casino.
- You cannot choose a successful active investment fund manager (mutual funds). They are very profitable... for fund managers and rarely for investors.

Rolf Dobelli,
The Art of Thinking Clearly: Better Thinking, Better Decisions (2013)

ETF's Exchange-Traded Funds (ETF's) - indextrackers

As the name suggests Exchange-Traded Funds are traded on exchanges, just like common stocks, and the other side of the trade is another investor like you, not the investment fund manager. Like mutual funds, ETFs offer investors a way to bundle their money into a fund that invests in shares, bonds or other assets.

Most ETFs are index tracking, which means that they try to match the performance and price movements of an index, such as the S&P 500, by putting together a portfolio that matches the index components as closely as possible.

Both mutual funds and ETFs hold portfolios of equities and/or bonds and sometimes slightly more exotic portfolios, such as precious metals or commodities, and both can also track indices but ETFs are more cost-effective and liquid because they are traded on exchanges as equities.

In addition to index tracking ETFs, there exist also low-cost, passively managed index tracking funds. These too are almost fully automated, track the index and are inexpensive. The difference lies mainly in their tradability. I think the differences are so small that I use them interchangeably. If I'm talking about an index tracker it can be an ETF but also an inexpensive passively managed fund.

To make things a bit more confusing there also exist actively managed ETFs not based on an index. Instead, they seek to achieve an investment objective by investing in a portfolio of stocks, bonds, and other assets. The handful of actively managed ETFs available are cheaper than actively managed investment funds.

Passive management is not the only reason why ETFs tend to be cheaper. Because buyers and sellers in an ETF do business with each other, managers have far less to do and in order to keep the ETF as close as possible to the intrinsic value of the index, as much as possible is done with a computer program, without any human intervention.

FIRE investors are generally long-term-oriented and rather risk-averse. A very good, inexpensive (cost-efficient) and easy way to diversify and therefore invest with a fairly limited risk is to limit yourself to investing in index trackers. In short, most FIRE investors stick to ETFs.

There are different types of ETFs to further diversify.

- Stock Index Trackers
- Real Estate Investment Trust index fund
- Bond Market index fund

In order to (easily and cost-effectively) diversify internationally, widely spread ETFs offer this possibility. This is why many FIRE investors have different ETFs in their portfolios with different regional focus.

Most FIRE investors follow a 3-fund or 4-fund portfolio strategy, also called a lazy portfolio strategy. The most common 3 or 4-fund portfolios include a bond ETF. The 4-fund portfolio that Vanguard is now employing consists of the following broad asset class index funds:

- Total U.S. stock market index fund
- Total international stock index fund
- Total U.S. bond index fund
- Total international bond index fund

When using iShares ETFs, investors can build a three-fund portfolio using:

- iShares Core S&P Total Market ETF (ITOT)
- iShares Core MSCI Total International Stock ETF (IXUS)
- iShares Core Total U.S. Bond Market ETF (AGG)

These obviously are well diversified but still very much focused on the US and they include a bond ETF which I personally don't want to include in my ETF portfolio.

If you think you are covered and best diversified with just the world-oriented ETFs, it's useful to understand how the spread of the ETF is geographically. If you are looking for global total market diversification you will find that World ETFs focus too much on a particular region, specifically the US, because the world's largest companies are American Tech funds.

In the case of ETFs with international coverage, it is advisable to find out about dividend leakage. Depending on the country in which a fund is domiciled and whether or not the country in question has made tax arrangements with your country, you will pay more or less tax on your dividend. In the Netherlands for example, the tax rate on dividends is 15%. In other countries this rate may be different. In the US, for example, it is 30%.

Let me explain with an example. If you live in the Netherlands, have a US share, investment fund or index fund that pays a dividend, 30% tax will be withheld on this dividend. The Netherlands has tax treaties with many countries. As a result, you usually don't have to pay more than the 15% tax that is applicable in the Netherlands. Excessively withheld dividend tax can usually be reclaimed through your tax return. However, if the Netherlands has no or no good tax treaty with a country, you may not be able to reclaim the withheld tax and pay more than 15%. In that case there will be a dividend leakage. The easiest way to circumvent this is to buy ETFs that are domiciled in the Netherlands.

Managing your portfolio

It may seem a bit overwhelming and unclear what choices to make. How much money will I deposit on a savings account and how much will I invest? Which shares or indexfunds do I need to buy? How often do I need to buy and sell? We will come to these questions soon. For now, it's good to define your investment goal: You want an investment strategy that aims to balance risk and return by dividing the assets of your portfolio according to your goals, risk tolerance and investment horizon.

When determining the amount you can invest, first answer the following questions:

What is my time horizon?

What is my risk tolerance (or risk aversion)?

Do I have debts?

How much of my assets, taking into account my savings and emergency fund, do I want to and can I invest?

What is my monthly savings amount? How much do I use to top up my savings and emergency fund, and how much do I want to invest each month?

Risk tolerance

In order to determine an investment strategy, consider how much risk suits you and your goals. Your risk tolerance can change over time and depends on your time horizon. Simply put, your risk tolerance is generally lower if you have less time to reach your goals and you may be able to afford a riskier portfolio at the beginning of your journey than at the end.

In the case of FIRE, at the end of your working life just before Financial Independence, you do not want to run the risk of the stock market collapsing so that you cannot stop working, or only much later. If you save and invest for a bucket list trip of one year for you and your family about 15 years from now, you might want to be a little more risk-tolerant and invest more aggressively in the first few years. But as the date approaches, you probably want to adopt a more risk-averse strategy and have a more conservative portfolio.

If your goal is more flexible, you can take more risk. For example, you might be willing to organize your bucket list trip in a different, more low-budget way when the return on your investments is not good. If you want to be able to use part of your FYM for a college fund for your children, it is probably better to take less risk.

How risk-tolerant are you?

What are my FYM and FIRE goals?

How concrete are my FYM and FIRE goals and how fixed are they in terms of the amount of money I need and when I need it?

To what extent am I willing to accept large fluctuations in my assets? What kind of downward deviation means I no longer sleep or I will not reach my goals?

To what extent do I have low-risk assets, such as a house, my savings accounts, my emergency fund in order? And can I survive without having to make a claim on my invested assets?

FYM and FIRE investors in general can be said to be risk-averse, cost-aware, they prefer to invest in well-diversified ETFs and focus on a fairly long-time horizon, they invest as a conservative investor.

Define your ETF investment strategy

ETFs allow you to customize your portfolio according to your defined goals. The variety is huge and most major banks and brokers offer dozens or even hundreds of different ETFs.

The most important choices are region focus and asset type.

Region:

- World
- Europe
- USA
- Asia
- Developed (developed)
- Developing (emerging)

Consisting of:

- Shares,
- Raw materials (especially gold and agriculture)
- Bonds (government bonds and corporate bonds)
- Real estate (residential mortgages, real estate companies).
- Other, including, for example, investing in inflation expectations or volatility

Find more information about the available ETFs and respective costs in your country. For example, the Financial Industry Regulatory Authority (FINRA) Fund Analyzer offers information and analysis on over 18,000 mutual funds, exchange traded funds (ETFs) and exchange traded notes (ETNs). This tool estimates the value of the funds and impact of fees and expenses on your investment and also gives you the ability to look up applicable fees and available discounts for funds: https://tools.finra.org/fund_analyzer/

For the Dutch the VEB has a nice portal https://www.veb.net/etf-portal with options to help you choose. In the overview of you can see what the costs are and you can filter and sort by costs and returns. Banks and brokers can also give you good information but they are less impartial.

How can I immediately start investing in ETFs?

You can say that there are two types of FIRE investors. The first group (I think the largest group) for whatever reason wants to have as little an active role as possible in investing. For example, because they are not interested in it, do not want to gain knowledge about it, or do not believe that an active role yields anything at all. For this group, the simplest safe portfolio strategy is to limit yourself to one to four ETFs that give you the diversification you want in terms of industry and region.

If you belong to the other group and you want to know more and you want to influence the development of your portfolio more, you will probably spend most of your time trying to figure out what you think is the best asset allocation for your goals. You can achieve the desired diversification yourself, not only geographically but also by industry and branches and even with non-equity ETFs.

Seven steps to your All World Portfolio

I'll explain how, in a simple and inexpensive way, to create your All World ETF Portfolio: a safe, balanced, globally diversified portfolio of index tracking funds. The goal is: buy and hold, or set and forget, meaning simplicity in the set-up of your portfolio, at low cost and then not have to worry about it anymore.

With this paragraph you can use the worksheet I have prepared and uploaded: fymfire.com/en/tools/#worldportfolio

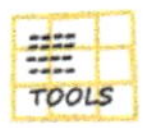

Use this worksheet to find the funds to create your All World Portfolio and calculate the amounts you want to invest.

I distinguish seven simple steps:

1. Decide which financial service provider you want to invest with. Take into consideration costs, convenience and reliability (or what you feel comfortable with).
2. Open your investment account.
3. Deposit the amount you want to invest now into your investment account.
4. Decide which ETF provider you want. This may depend on your choice in step 1. Not all indextrackers and ETFs are available with all banks/brokers or in countries.
5. Determine your Total World Portfolio. Here you choose whether or not to include Small Caps, whether or not to include Europe and whether or not to deviate from the standard percentages.
6. Determine the amounts you want to invest in the various ETFs depending on the funds you have available and the percentages.
7. Place your orders.

Nothing can go wrong and you can change everything later. If at any time you want a different variant than the one you have chosen in step 5, you can do so by making additional purchases. If you want to invest with other amounts periodically, you can adjust the amounts in your automatic money transfer and purchase order. If you temporarily do not want to invest periodically at all, you can revoke the periodic purchase order and money transfer.

Step 1 - Determine which financial service provider you want to invest with.

You can choose from: your own bank, another bank, another asset manager or a specialized (online) broker.

For many novice investors the current house bank is the most trusted financial institution. Major banks offer excellent investment accounts. Opening an investment account is easy. You can buy the most popular index-tracking funds and ETFs from no or low transaction costs in order to take advantage of the low costs of those ETFs and maintain an All World ETF portfolio. Periodic (automatic) purchases are possible and usually cost nothing extra. The costs of investing with your own bank are at least very competitive compared to the well-known brokers and often the costs at the banks are lower.

The costs of investing can be broken down into:

1. Basic services
    - Fixed costs of the investment account
    - Variable costs: the service fee is a percentage of the investments.
2. Transaction costs: you do not pay any transaction costs to the banks for buying or selling index funds.
3. Costs of the fund managers.

The differences between the final costs of the different banks are very small. As far as I'm concerned the differences are not big enough to switch to another bank if you are otherwise satisfied with your bank.

For an investment account with a bank, you need an ordinary bank account, which costs money. Taking an extra bank account just because a bank offers a cheap investment account does not make much sense.

You may have your reason for choosing a broker. A broker is an intermediary in stock trading. The main reason for wanting to use a broker is probably convenience. With some brokers you can opt for one comprehensive global fund. You don't have to decide for yourself in what ratio you want to keep the different ETFs and you don't have to keep an eye on whether this ratio changes over time and whether you need to make adjustments. They simply use the same ETFs you can buy yourself and they charge a fee for this service.

As far as I'm concerned brokers do not offer an advantage but they do offer higher costs. The different options and costs of the banks and brokers available to you is something you should research in your own country. For more active investors, features such as trading/transaction speed, a helpdesk, a user-friendly online interface and the low transaction costs for trading individual shares offered by specialized brokers might be important. For passive ETF investors I don't find this relevant and a broker is not worth the eventual higher costs of ETFs. If you would like to invest in individual shares at a later stage you can open an additional investment account with a broker, specifically for your shares, probably free of charge.

You should not be guided in this choice by temporary offers. An entry bonus or transaction fee credit does not have enough impact on your total costs and return in the long term. Once you've made your choice you can of course see if you can make use of an offer or promotion. Check out your provider's website or the multitude of blogs on the subject, but don't get distracted.

Step 2 - Open your trading account.

Opening an investment account is very easy with all providers and speaks for itself.

Step 3 - Deposit to your trading account the amount you want to invest now.

You don't have to deposit more money into the trading account than you need and you can buy ETFs for any amount you have in mind. This is the easiest with the index tracking funds where you can choose any amount. If you want to deposit $250 once, that's fine. If you want to invest $100,000 this month you can. If you only want to invest periodically then you do not need to deposit money into the trading account because you will set up a periodic transfer to the value of the monthly amount to be invested.

Step 4 - Decide which ETF provider you want.

If you have chosen a bank or broker find out which low cost index trackers / ETFs they offer. Choose a provider of ETF's like iShares, EMIM, IUSN or Vanguard.

Step 5 - Determine your All World Portfolio.

The goal is to build and maintain an All World ETF Portfolio. This can easily be achieved by purchasing two, three or four ETFs.

2 fund portfolio		3 fund portfolio		4 fund portfolio	
World	88%	World	78%	World	70%
Emerging Marketss	12%	Emerging Markets	12%	Emerging Markets	10%
		Small Caps	10%	Small Caps	10%
				Europe	10%

The percentages are determined on the basis of market capitalization. The percentages are an approximation, they are not 100% fixed and as far as I'm concerned the exactness doesn't really matter and you can always adjust in the future.

With an investment in a World Index tracker like NT World (or iShares Core MSCI World or Vanguard Total Stock Market) you buy a basket of shares in about 1600 large and medium-sized companies in 23 developed countries of the world. The most important developed countries in which investments are made are: United States, Japan, United Kingdom, France and Switzerland. A very large proportion of the investments are in the five largest companies in America: Apple, Microsoft, Amazon, Facebook and Google.

With an investment in an Emerging Markets fund you buy a basket of shares in about 3000 large, medium and small companies in 26 developing countries. The main developing countries in which investments are made are: China, Taiwan, South Korea, India and Brazil.

By adding a World Small Cap fund to your portfolio, you can buy a basket of over 4,000 smaller companies in 23 developed countries (with more than half invested in the United States). This means more diversification, also by industry. These stocks and therefore the fund are more volatile, which means that there is a chance of higher returns, but also a higher risk (chance of lower returns).

By adding a Europe fund to your portfolio you buy a basket of more than 400 large and medium sized companies in 15 developed European countries (especially the United Kingdom, France, Germany, Switzerland and the Netherlands). My personal reason for having a preference for adding the NT Europe fund is more diversification and less dependence on the economic situation in the United States and China.

Note: this last variant deviates from the desire to follow the world-wide index as much as possible. It does, however, fit in with the desire to invest in as many companies worldwide as possible. This type of portfolio build-up means that you think you are doing better than the market by giving a specific region more weighting than in the global index.

Choose variant 1, 2 or 3.

Step 6 - Determine the amounts you want to invest in the different ETFs

You have determined in step 3 how much you want to invest now or periodically. You have chosen a variant in step 5 and can now use the percentages. Simply multiply your amount by the percentage and you have your budget per ETF. You can also use a very simple spreadsheet for this (fymfire.com/en/tools/#worldportfolio). It is possible that there's a minimum amount per purchase with your bank or broker.

Step 7 - Place your orders

In order to start investing periodically, for example per month, you need to add this to your order. In addition, you have to make sure that there is enough money in your deposit account. You can do this by setting up an automatic transfer from your bank account to your investment account in the amount of the total monthly amount.

Buying ETFs or placing orders in your online banking/investment account:
(Every bank and broker has a different user-interface and process but most probably ordering your ETFs goes something like this).

1. Log in and go to your investment account
2. Click on 'new order
3. In the menu choose ETFs. Look for (part of) the name of the ETF, the ISIN code (see the #worldportfolio spreadsheet) of the fund or scroll through the list. Click on the desired ETF.
4. Click on 'buy'.

5. Enter your order. Decide whether you want to place a one-time or periodic order. Enter the amount you calculated in step 6 above. Or calculate the number of ETFs you want to buy by dividing your calculated budget by the price of the ETF.
6. Check the order summary, adjust if necessary. Approve the order / confirm if you want to place the order.
7. You can see the status of your order. It may take a while before your order is processed. For some index funds or ETFs it may take a few working days before you see the 'executed' status.

In the following paragraphs I will share more detailed information about the components mentioned above. If the above is enough information for now, you can skip the following text and go to 'And now sit back'.

Even if you want to spend as little time and effort as possible and want a portfolio that is as simple as possible, you define at least once a personal investment strategy with which you find that you have sufficient spread.

How do I know which ETFs are available and which ones to choose? What is the best way to buy ETFs? This depends on a few things:

- Where do you have your bank accounts or do you already invest? At which bank or broker?
- Which provider of ETFs do you prefer?
- What spread do you want to achieve?

Which bank or broker

You can invest via your bank or via a separate online broker. If you choose to actively invest in more than just a few ETFs, an online broker might be the best option, for example because you want to find the lowest transaction costs for the transactions you intend to do and who is charging the lowest management costs.

If you only want to invest in ETFs and don't want to have to do much with them, you can look at what your bank offers in terms of investment accounts. I think most banks offer online trading through their brokerage arm and offer the option 'Self Investing' so you don't pay for investment management. The costs of opening the account and buying and selling ETFs, especially if you already have a bank account, can be minimal or even zero and you may have the option of investing automatically (free of charge) in the ETFs you want via your bank.

Be aware of aggressive marketing. There exist quite a large number of affiliate programs and you may come across many blogs and websites that offer you deals to open an account; just be aware that they may be influenced by the broker and they may not give you a complete overview of all providers.

(and just to be clear: I do not advise you to make certain choices and I do not participate in affiliate programs of a bank, broker, financial product or service).

Which ETF provider?

There are several companies offering ETFs; well-known names are iShares, Vanguard, State Street SPDR and Northern Trust (NT being especially of interest to Dutch investors). You decide which ETF you want and you check yourself which ETFs your bank or broker offers. If you really don't care, you find the ETF that is the least expensive or best available at your bank or broker.

How do you want to spread?

If you want to build a simple ETF portfolio, you will already have achieved diversification by investing in ETFs of shares in large companies in the US, Europe or the whole World. This gives you a basket of shares in companies in different industries in the US, Europe or around the world. You can also decide if you want to include Asian or developing countries.

Please note that World ETFs consist of shares in the largest companies in the world. Because the largest companies in the world are largely American Tech companies, the United States region is often over-represented in a World ETF.

You can easily build a portfolio from a number of ETFs. You can make a choice for yourself and come up with percentages with which you think you can build a nice portfolio. Then you can set your own budget. You calculate how much money you want to buy ETFs for and you put in your orders. Once your ETFs have been purchased, you don't have to look at them anymore. If you want to make monthly purchases, you can do this in exactly the same way according to the percentages you have defined. Depending on your bank or broker you can also buy ETFs automatically (free of charge) on a monthly basis for a predefined amount of money.

How do you make up the percentages for your ETF investment mix?

This is quite arbitrary and personal. If you want your results to depend as little as possible on your own ideas, because you have no idea, investing in an optimal mix of globally spread ETFs is the easiest.

The most popular mix to achieve this is the one that follows as balanced as possible the entire world economy through the ratio of about 75% developed countries, 12% emerging countries, 13% small businesses (small caps).

You can also choose to expand this with Europe and buy for example 50% world, 25% Europe, 12% emerging countries (emerging markets), 13% small companies (small caps).

If you really don't know and don't have any idea about it, it doesn't matter right? You can change the proportions in the future if you want. If you want to limit yourself to one ETF you just find an ETF that follows the MSCI World index, which is the best-known global index. iShares, Vanguard, HSBC, BNP Paribas, NT and probably all other ETF companies have one following the MSCI World Index.

I've made this easy for myself and I don't have the intention to deviate from this in the future. I have three different ETFs: Europe, World and Emerging Markets. That's it.

- 50% World: Northern Trust World Custom ESG Equity Index: The investment objective is to closely match the risk and return characteristics of the MSCI World Custom ESG Index, with reinvestment of the net dividends.
- 25% Europe: Northern Trust Europe Custom ESG Index FGR: The objective of the Fund is to closely monitor the risk and return characteristics of the MSCI Europe Index, reinvesting the net dividend.
- 25% Emerging Markets: Northern Trust Emerging Markets Custom ESG Equity Index: The fund aims to match the risk and return characteristics of the MSCI Emerging Markets Custom ESG Index as closely as possible, excluding companies that do not meet socially responsible standards.

What does an ETF or index tracker look like?

You can find more information about ETFs via banks and brokers or the ETF company directly, for example in a prospectus, fact sheet or annual report. It quickly becomes quite technical but you may find it interesting to look at the objectives and the investment policy, a risk and return profile, the costs and the results achieved in the past.

In the fact sheet you can see the size of the fund but also quite specifically the breakdown into funds, subsectors and regions/countries. As a result, you can see that a World ETF has shares of the largest companies in the world and as a result, as I mentioned earlier, is strongly over-represented in the region 'United States' and the subsector 'Tech industry'. This is due to the heavy weights of the large American companies Apple, Microsoft Corporation, Amazon.com, Facebook, Alphabet Inc. (Google) and Johnson & Johnson.

That is why, as mentioned earlier, I am holding the ETFs Emerging Markets and Europe. The developing countries in which I invest through the Emerging Markets ETF are China, Taiwan, Korea, India, South Africa, Brazil, Saudi Arabia, Russia, Thailand and Malaysia and through the Europe ETFs I invest mainly in the Financials, Consumer Staples, Healthcare, Industrials, Consumer Discretionary subsectors.

On the MSCI website overviews are available of all parts of the indexes with all weights up to six decimal places. If you look at NT Europe Custom ESG Index, for example, you can see the enormous diversity of well-known and less well-known companies in all conceivable industries and branches.

Once you have decided which ETF to invest in, you can easily find the ISIN number on the internet or in the factsheet and use it in your online trading platform at your bank or broker to make the purchase.

MSCI website with the index constituents
www.msci.com/constituents

And now sit back?

Yep, you're in it for the long term, so you don't have to deal with short-term fluctuations. This might feel a bit tricky, and it remains uncomfortable if you see your total portfolio amount decrease for a few days in a row, or if you end up in a huge dip or even crash. You can even choose not to really look at your portfolio at all. For the performance of your portfolio it does not matter whether or not you keep an eye on it.

I'm going to try to reassure you and explain to you that the best strategy here is: don't do anything, don't touch, don't sell and don't panic.

If you make regular purchases or automatic deposits, it's even interesting to keep doing so in a declining market.

No panic?

Thorough research has been conducted into the effect of fluctuations, movements, dips and crashes on the long-term development of the market as a whole and of indices in particular. Look, if the (financial) world really collapses, your money is no longer of any use to you. Hopefully you then have a house where you can live and for the rest you have to see if you can arrange food and essentials through barter. In all other cases it is important that you have your emergency fund in order and available, and the chance that your invested assets evaporate before you die is very, very small. There are all kinds of models based on periods when crashes and upturns alternate, and the general conclusion is that in the long run you are safe with a return expectation of 4%. In most cases your return will be higher, on average towards the 7% to 8% but with the conservative 4% percentage it is safe to calculate.

There will be market downturns and crashes but markets will bounce back as well. If you are able to keep buying in a declining and cheap period, your average purchase price will only get lower and you will benefit more from a downturn than if you stopped buying.

The effect of selling for a lower price during such a dip, I hope I don't have to talk about, right? To get to the same portfolio value as before the dip, you need to make up for your loss by making new purchases at a lower price than your selling price, and you, like everyone else, will most likely not be able to time the market.

If it's not quite clear yet, think about the sales price development of a house. The development of the value of your house has no direct effect on your monthly expenses (except for example value-based taxes). If the value of your house has risen significantly, you will only benefit if you sell and only then. And even if the value of your house drops, you only lose money when you sell, so you stay put if you can. This is also the case with investing, not selling, not panicking, buying cheaply if you can.

If you belong to the group of FIRE investors who wants to be more active in investing, you will have to study more in the beginning, explore all the options, find out why different investors make different choices, think for yourself what you think is the best portfolio to achieve your goals. You invest for the long term but you can make tactical shifts in your portfolio in response to new insights, changing preferences or market movements, such as the level of interest rates or long-term effects of macro-economic events or geopolitical incidents or power shifts. You understand that the more you intervene, adjust and deviate from the largest basket of companies, the index, the more fluctuations you can expect and thus increase the risk.

Investing in other types of assets

Micro investing - Crowdfunding

Crowdfunding is an opportunity for entrepreneurs who are not listed on the stock exchange and cannot issue shares to raise money from an otherwise inaccessible market, i.e. the private investor. There are two types of crowdfunding: equity crowdfunding and reward-based crowdfunding.

Equity crowdfunding

With equity crowdfunding you invest in the growth of a mostly young company and get 'shares' for it. These shares are worth nothing if the company does not grow or goes bankrupt. You can usually not count on dividends and the shares are not freely negotiable, which makes it difficult to get out at a good time. Having said that, it is possible to help a young company grow and if it is well organized you can count on a good return.

I especially liked the idea of having a share in the Brewdog brewery from the UK. There are all kinds of advantages for you as a crowdfunder, and at the time I lived near a Brewdog pub. The crowdfunding program of Brewdog is called Brewdog Equity for Punks. It's very popular, quite overfunded. They have raised a total of about 95 million dollars so far. I never got into it in the end.

Reward based crowdfunding

With reward-based crowdfunding, such as Kickstarter, you're usually the first to get the product the company you're investing in is developing, if it ever comes to it. And then you just have to wait and see if the product is worth it. If you use it to help someone write a book or develop a special sneaker, that's just great fun. Again, you can help someone with a good idea enormously, but it is not really intended or suitable to grow your FYM or FIRE pot.

You may wonder why a company doesn't take this money from a bank and as far as I'm concerned, the most likely explanation is that the banks don't want to take this risk.

Microcredit, microfinance, microlending

Peer to peer lending' is also gaining popularity with platforms such as Mintos and Kiva. These are personal loans to a private person but also to a company or even a charity. I think it is a nice development but as far as I am concerned it is too risky to take along as a serious option with FYM or FIRE investing and not interesting for three reasons.

1. It is not well known yet how many borrowers stop paying back. This may be due to a limited track record. It seems that with some platforms this is quite a real risk.
2. There is a lot of promotion and through affiliate marketing especially where the referrers make money from your new application.
3. The costs charged by the P2P platforms reduce your return on investment.

Pay attention to this when you read an enthusiastic story about any platform.

I strongly believe in the social usefulness of microfinance in developing countries. A small investment, i.e. a relatively small amount of money for someone from a developed country, can make the difference for an entrepreneur in a developing country. Melinda Gates writes about this in an inspiring way. I see this more as development aid than as an opportunity to invest with FYM and FIRE in mind.

Kiva is a great concept which focuses entirely on non-profit borrowers. The idea is that through Kiva, which itself is a non-profit organization, you help people all over the world to finance their business without interest. As a lender, you can choose to lend money to people in different categories, including loans for single parents, people in conflict areas or companies that focus on food or health. Without interest for the borrower, also means 0% interest for the investor. Your FYM or FIRE goal does not come any closer. Maybe something to do at the moment you are FIRE.

Melinda Gates, The Moment of Lift:
How Empowering Women Changes the World (2019)

Real estate - your home

For me, the best investments I have ever made have been the investments in my home. My partner and I bought the apartment, we completely renovated it and invested in a substantial extension of the apartment with an extra master bedroom and an extra living room so that the house became more suitable for renting out to an expat family. We also made additional repayments and refinanced for a few percent lower interest so that our monthly costs became lower. Furthermore, the market has done its job and the increase in the value of our property over the past few years was 8% on average, every year, so the value has more than doubled in ten years. At the moment we do not live in this apartment and we may never live there again. For us it is more than ever an investment.

Rent or Buy?

Renting a house versus owning a house. A much-discussed topic amongst FIRE investors probably everywhere in the world. There is not really one strategic best choice when it comes to growing FYM and FIRE money and it really depends on your personal situation and the country or even the city you live in.

Renting a house does not seem to be an investment strategic choice but if you can achieve lower costs by renting and invest the money you have left over, it may be.

Whether you are going to rent or buy the house where you live is an important decision. Not only does it affect how much money you have left at the end of the month, it also affects your lifestyle and the amount of wealth and savings you build up over the years.

Owning is not always better than renting, and renting is not always easier than owning. Contrary to what is often thought and said, renting does not mean that you 'throw money away' every month if this leaves you with more money to save and invest, for example. And possession doesn't always build wealth 'in the long run' if you can't pay off enough, if your house decreases in value and if the value evaporates from the money you've invested in things you consider valuable but someone else does not.

Rent

Renting offers flexibility, predictable monthly expenses and someone who handles and pays for repairs. You can move free of charge every time your lease expires, at any point in time with a notice period. When you rent, you know exactly how much you're going to spend on housing each month. This also allows you to know exactly how much you have left and how much you are saving. Depending on the rules in your country, you may have to deal with unpredictable rent increases. Try to make this as predictable as possible in your contract.

You never have to pay for repairs and maintenance, for example, when replacing a roof. You also don't have to deal with the hassle, you don't have to do any chores, you have nothing to do with leaseholder meetings.

An important reason for renting as part of growing your FYM and FIRE assets is that you can live somewhere at the lowest possible total monthly cost. You can invest the money you have left over. You may be able to build up more capital with this than with a rise in the value of a house you own.

Buy

Home ownership brings immaterial benefits, such as a sense of stability and pride in your property. In addition, you can benefit from increases in value and tax benefits. Owning your own home does make most people inflexible. You can't just sell it if you want to live elsewhere more cheaply or if house prices drop and you see the value of your property evaporate.

Almost every owner will eventually see an increase in value in the longer term. But in the meantime, there are considerable fluctuations and dips and eventually your house can also lose value. A lot of value. The development of the neighborhood or the departure of a large employer can all have an impact, both positive and negative.

As with renting, you actually need to look at the total cost of home ownership very rationally and these are usually higher than the total rental cost. If these total costs do not include mortgage repayments, you will save less than when you rent.

Another disadvantage is that your money is stuck. You cannot withdraw money temporarily. An advantage is that at the end of the ride, for example when you become FI or retire, you can sell your house or take out a reverse mortgage and use your money to pay for costs of living.

The moment you are able to gain a passive income from your property, through renting it out, this changes the story. If you can use the rental income to cover all your costs and gain some passive income, you are on your way to FI.

Tip

A final advantage of owning a home is the effect of almost imperceptibly reducing your debt and therefore growing your wealth by making extra repayments. While it is difficult for many people to save, it's rather easy to increase monthly repayments. After all, the monthly mortgage is the most important bill that has to be paid. If you automatically set up a monthly extra repayment it feels like you are living more expensively but in fact you are saving money for later, that you are not spending on other things now.

So ... rent or buy?

Which option is best for your situation is completely personal. It depends on your personal situation and is not only about money but also about comfort, emotion and your vision of your life and your chosen lifestyle. If you want to be honest with yourself and your priority is to reach your FYM and FIRE goals, when choosing to rent or buy you can finally consider what you think the effect of lifestyle inflation is on your total cost. Hardly anyone is immune to lifestyle inflation, so it's advisable to think about this in time.

My opinion is that the negative financial effect (it costs you more money) of lifestyle inflation in the case of owning your home (where you live, so not as an object to let) can be greater than in the case of renting your home. My idea and experience is that you incur considerable costs because you are more inclined to upgrade your own property than the landlord would be. You also tend to do this more often than a landlord would think necessary. As an owner, you do spend money on non-essential things, whereas your landlord does not.

Investments such as home automation, gadgets, rain showers, grill plates and a fireplace are beautiful and important for your enjoyment but as an investment (almost) worthless. When selling, the buyer is the first to pull out everything because it's too old and dirty and no longer meets the now changed lifestyle wishes.

Pulling your money out of your house

For many people who reach retirement age their house is a large part of their household assets. Because you have repaid the mortgage your whole life, living in your home now costs you almost nothing. Because of these low costs, you can use the income from your investments to cover the cost of living.

Reaching your FI moment and stopping with paid work can also mean that you want to live somewhere else, for example because you are no longer dependent on commuting and want to live outside the city, or in the city, or in another region far away from your work. The option of moving offers an interesting option if you live in a relatively spacious house, for example, with vacant bedrooms of the children who are out of the house or in an expensive location.

I think it's an interesting idea to sell your property and search and buy another smaller and cheaper property for let's say half of the amount selling the house yields. You can use the other half of the proceeds from the sale of your home to pay for your FI life expenses. When you buy your new home, you can take into account your new living wishes that suit this phase in your life. Finally, you can even take into account your wish to sell this house again when you reach retirement age, if desired.

If you don't want to move you cannot really pull out the money invested in your house, it's an illiquid asset. However, you can still get your hands on some of that capital. You can take out a reverse mortgage on your existing home. Reverse mortgage loans allow homeowners to convert their home equity into cash income with no monthly mortgage payments.

Depending on the personal situation and the possibilities and limitations of the mortgage provider, it is possible to take up between 25% and around 65% of the value of the property.

The downside to a reverse mortgage loan is that you are using your home's equity while you are alive. After you pass, your heirs will receive less of an inheritance. Another possible downside would be regrets by taking a reverse mortgage too early in your retirement years.

The high costs of reverse mortgages are not worth it for some people. You're better off selling your home and moving to another place if that's what you want and if that does not make your monthly expenses explode because of high rent.

Pay off a mortgage or invest?

For a long time there was a clear preference within the FIRE community for paying off debts as quickly as possible, whatever the debt, including mortgage. I think the low interest rate nowadays (2020) has changed this for some.

Repayment reduces your monthly costs. However, you cannot quickly reduce the cost of your mortgage by repayment if you don't pay a lot of interest. Investing the money could be more profitable. Make the calculation for yourself with your financial details. If you have the choice between repayment of $50,000 or investing $50,000, what is more profitable? Depending on your mortgage type, conditions and especially the interest rate, you can expect to benefit more by investing your money now and repaying the mortgage later.

If you rent out a house, paying off or refinancing to lower the interest rate and paying for improvements to the rental property itself without borrowing money seems like a good investment. If you can lower the costs of the loan and/or increase the income from renting out because you can ask a better price for the improved rental house your passive income will increase.

Simply put, you have to weigh the repayment of a mortgage against the (possible) return prospects of other options. If you have an unusually high interest rate on your mortgage, it makes financial sense to first repay the debt or refinance to lower the interest rate.

I suspect that most people opt for a combination of both extra repayment and investment. It also depends on what phase of the mortgage (period) you are in and it can be more attractive to repay extra in the first phase of your mortgage so that you benefit from this for a longer period of time, regardless of what the market and the interest rate will do in the future. But you can also say that at the beginning of your mortgage it is better to invest your money so that it can grow for as long as possible, as long as the interest rate of the mortgage remains much lower as the possible return on your investments.

Leveraging real estate

If you really want to grow your money with real estate, you'll have to do something with it. One possibility is leveraging, using the leverage of borrowed capital to increase the return on your investment.

1. Buy a property, preferably one that reduces your monthly costs, put your savings aside.
2. Buy a second home, keep the first one, rent out the first one.
3. As long as your cash flow from your passive income, i.e. the rental income, increases because the rent you receive covers all costs, you can still buy and rent out another house. The increase in value of the property also helps. This is leveraging and a way to reach your FI goal faster.

You can repeat this a few times depending on your situation. But first do your own research and get help from experts.

Chapter 14
Achieve

For most people reading about FIRE, the words 'congratulations, you have achieved FIRE!' are still a long way off.

Points of attention for this phase are:

- Live your FIRE life. Enjoy being time rich.
- Redesign your new financially independent lifestyle
- Recalibrate your goals, your budgets, withdrawal strategy and spending behavior.
- Experiment with your new lifestyle with lots of time, freedom and quality.
- Monitor your lifestyle and finances, evaluate, celebrate successes, adjust where necessary.

Have a good day. Live your life. Enjoy the time.

This is of course what it is all about. I think the challenge of this phase is to live according to the lifestyle you have designed and to keep looking for ways to make it more beautiful, more fun, easier, more comfortable within your own boundaries. Keep evaluating whether you are on the right path or off the path, and whether that matters.

This is the phase of harvesting: You let your money work for you, and you pay the things you always wanted to do from your own resources. You can stop working and are no longer dependent on an employer or the government for your income.

This may be the time for a redesign of your new Financial Independent (FI) lifestyle. Maybe it will be a lot easier now that you have the time. Maybe you can think of even more ways to live Smarter, Better, Cheaper and again make smart choices and decisions that allow you to live a comfortable, free life without the need to work for it any longer.

You can look again at your strategy and system for this phase, and your spending plan (burn-rate), savings and investment strategy and withdrawal targets. It might just be that you look at things differently now or that you can or want to do it with more or less money than you had previously thought.

What are you going to do with the Gift of Time? I think almost all FIRE people know how to fill their days well. There are a lot of people who finally have the time to read the books they always have wanted to read or to spend more time with their family, children, grandchildren and partner. People help others or take the time to enjoy the best movies or series that have appeared in the last decade. People start cooking extensively or finally shape up the garden. People try new things and spend time outdoors a lot.

There are examples of FI people who travel half of the year while spending the other half of the year at home, as much time as possible with family. There are FI people who work as volunteers or set something up themselves. There are FI people who do more sports than ever, cycling, longer walks, hours of golf, rowing, sailing, you name it. There are FI people who wander around flea markets or gem fairs for days. There are FI people who buy a camper van and travel for months in a row. There are FI people who spend the winter in a country where the weather is nice, and where it is often a lot cheaper to live comfortably. There are (many) FI people who learn new things, study philosophy, learn cooking, baking, do photography course, learn Visual Basic in Excel, start scuba diving, get their motorcycle license, go skydiving, do yoga, it doesn't matter.

Even though for most people it is rather difficult to do nothing at all, it is wonderful not to have to do anything. I'm not getting bored at all. I read a lot. I listen to a lot of podcasts. I am outdoors a lot. Because I have so much time on my hands, I spend much more time on activities like groceries shopping and cooking. I now make my own (Indian) bread and pizza dough. I never managed to fit a physical work-out into my daily routine, now I'm standing on an exercise mat (almost) every day accompanied by an online work-out video.

We walk every day for an hour and often longer. We spend time together and chat on the way. We see all kinds of things, which we would never have seen if we hadn't been walking. We do more shopping at small local stores and hardly ever visit the supermarket. We like to support local entrepreneurs and it is nice to get to know the people and have a chat. It is the least efficient way of shopping but it doesn't matter now, it is more fun and good for body and mind. I can enjoy 'the moment' much more, I enjoy my surroundings, the weather, nature, the view. We are time-rich, and this feels great.

For many, this part of their lives is also about giving back to the community, be it knowledge, skills or time. It feels good to help others without needing anything in return. My wife participated in a Yoga Teacher Training Course last year, mainly because she's passionate about yoga but also so she might be able to do something with it in the future. As soon as we arrived in Goa, we met people who asked her to teach yoga classes at the resort they run. My wife grabbed that opportunity with both hands.

This obviously didn't feel like work, even though my wife takes this kind of work very seriously. This is really something quite different from the stressful international marketing manager role at one of the largest companies in the world she had before.

I recently helped a young entrepreneur set up social media to promote his bakery. He has always worked in kitchens and bakeries and is very good at his job and now he started his own business. He makes great bread, brownies and cakes but he doesn't know anything about information technology and social media. I enjoy spending some of my time setting up his account and creating and posting messages and photos. It is almost no effort for me, and it goes without saying that I don't charge a fee for this. This doesn't feel like work either but the satisfaction I experience when I see his big smile, and the enormous gratitude he expresses when a post on his Facebook page gets more than 200 likes, is priceless.

I also helped an entrepreneurial couple by discussing a disagreement with their local business partner. I looked into their administration and discussed this with their business partner. While, in my pre-FIRE life, I would have asked at least a few hundred euros for this, I could now do this as a friendship service and received, besides praise and thanks, a few drinks and a few nights in their resort.

We have been looking at and discussing about an opportunity to manage a guesthouse on one of the islands of the Maldives in the future. The guesthouse is on an island where whale sharks and manta rays regularly swim nearby. My wife can teach yoga classes to the guests and maybe even pro bono to the locals. I might be able to reactivate my divemaster status and guide diving guests. Because we have a passive income stream and sufficient FYM we can say a resounding yes to such opportunities even if it’s unclear if we can ever expect any income in return.

In this phase I think it is also important to think about how things are going, to evaluate and adjust where necessary. What went well, what could be better or different? Can you enjoy more by spending more time on something? Is it easier to spend less now that you have the time? Do you experience that there are many things that you no longer need at all that you found important in your previous life? Do you feel that you are on the right track? Which goals, dreams or ambitions do you need to adjust?

Keep 2.0

Recalibrate your goals, your budgets, and redesign your spending plan to match the new income stream. Just as you did during the accumulation (Get), retention (Keep) and growth (Grow) of your wealth, you can budget at this stage so that your money doesn't run out before the end of the month, for your new situation and with your new disposable income.

You let your money work for you and you pay for your freedom and the things you always wanted to do with your own money. Your withdrawal strategy, withdrawing part of your assets to pay for the costs of living, is important and fundamentally different in the phase of withdrawal than in the phase of capital growth. You determined your withdrawal strategy earlier when you thought about how much money you would need and when you wanted to stop working. This moment has now arrived and now you can recalibrate your withdrawal strategy.

Take a snapshot of your total asset situation and determine, again, your withdrawal, tax and investment strategy. What were your starting points? What has changed in the (financial) world and in your life, and what do you have to take into account? What has changed for yourself, your ideas, wishes, plans and what consequences does that have?

One of the most important considerations is to create a new risk profile for yourself and adjust your investment portfolio accordingly. You probably want to run less risk and there is probably also less need to take risk. You probably need more certainty that you can pay for your life without having to go back to work in case of disappointing results of your investment portfolio.

Choose your lifestyle again and enjoy

Think about the lifestyle you want, and what you can afford. Think about the impact of quitting work on the needs you have. What can you stop, what do you want to start, what can you do differently, what do you want to keep?

Do you want to live smaller or elsewhere?

Smaller houses are cheaper to rent, buy or maintain than large houses. Downsizing also offers the opportunity to clean up and declutter, get rid of stuff you no longer need.

Think about where and how you want to live. Do you want to move to an apartment or flat? Do you want to live somewhere else, in the city or just outside it? Do you want to live a nomadic life, live in a warm country for part of the year, travel around in a camper van or on a sailing boat? Can you rent out your apartment during the periods you don't live in your house yourself?

You are now time-rich

Think about how you want to deal with the gift of time. You are now time-rich, what can you do with this?

More time to move yourself

Think again about transport needs you now might have. At least for work you don't have to go out anymore. You have much more time to do all the other things you want to do and to visit all the places you have wanted to. This can be a good time to get rid of your car or buy a more economical, compact vehicle.

More time to prepare your meals

The best way to economize on food is to eat at home and cook for yourself. If this wasn't a hobby yet, try to make it a hobby now that you have a lot of time and can pay a lot of attention to healthy, tasty and affordable food.

You also have a lot more time to do your shopping and you might be able to buy smarter, for example at a market only open during the day.

More time to work on your health

Get and stay fit by walking or cycling regularly. Do your shopping while walking as much as possible. Walking is free and an excellent way to stay fit. If you spend a lot of time at home, it's a good habit to add some exercise to your daily routine. Adding half an hour of workout every morning makes a big difference. You can find all kinds of support online, for example on YouTube, to keep you motivated. Have a look at online bodyweight workouts to get you started, all you need is a fitness mat.

More time for entertainment

Create a 'To Read' list in your To Do app and finally read the books you never got around to. Create a 'To Watch' list and watch the series you never had the time for. Visit museums, art galleries and live performances in the park. Find a study online or an open university for adults, learn new things.

More time to help others

Whatever your knowledge, skills and experience, you can offer help to whoever you meet in this phase of your life. You can probably help others enormously with your hobby or passion. You can work as a volunteer. There are online platforms for volunteering in your own country but also abroad.

Good luck and have fun with your journey from Fuck You Money to FIRE. Keep me informed if you want.

Merijn Heijnen

Books consulted and recommended

BJ Fogg, Tiny Habits - The Small Changes That Change Everything (2019)

Bronnie Ware, Top Five Regrets of the Dying: A Life Transformed by the Dearly Departing (2019)

Cait Flanders, The Year of Less: How I Stopped Shopping, Gave Away My Belongings, and Discovered Life is Worth More Than Anything You Can Buy in a Store

Daniel Gilbert, Stumbling on Happiness (2007)

David Bach & John David Mann, The Latte Factor - Why You Don't Have to Be Rich to Live Rich (2019)

David Graeber, Bullshit Jobs: The Rise of Pointless Work, and What We Can Do About It (2018)

Elizabeth Warren, All Your Worth: The Ultimate Lifetime Money Plan (2005)

Greg Harvey, Microsoft Excel 2019 for Dummies

Hanneke van Veen Rob van Eeden, Your Money or Your Life

Hector Garcia en Francesc Miralles, Ikigai: The Japanese Secret to a Long and Happy Life (2017)

Jacob Lund Fisker, Early Retirement Extreme: A Philosophical and Practical Guide to Financial Independence (2010)

Jim Collins, Good to Great: Why Some Companies Make the Leap...And Others Don't

Melinda Gates, The Moment of Lift: How Empowering Women Changes the World (2019)

Michael Alexander, Microsoft Excel VBA for Dummies

Patrick Rhone, enough (2016)

Robert and Edward Skidelski, How Much is Enough? (2013)

Rolf Dobelli, The Art of Thinking Clearly (2013)

Simon Sinek, Start with Why: How Great Leaders Inspire Everyone to Take Action (2011)

Stephen R. Covey, The 7 Habits of Highly Effective People (2010)

Timothy Ferriss, The 4-Hour Workweek: Escape 9-5, Live Anywhere, and Join the New Rich (2009)

Vicki Robin and Joe Dominguez, Your Money or Your Life: 9 Steps to Transforming Your Relationship with Money and Achieving Financial Independence (1992); updated (2018)

About the author

In his pre-FIRE life, Merijn Heijnen worked for various companies as a management consultant, workshop facilitator and team leader. He is an innovative and creative thinker and passionate speaker and writer.

His greatest passion is travelling. He has visited about 90 countries during his travels and still has a long wish list.
He lived and worked in Amsterdam and London before leaving, with his wife Judith, on a trip that would last 3.5 years.
From full time travelers they turned into expats, with a permanent place to live as long as the visa allows. At the time of writing they live in Goa, India.

If you're curious where we are at the moment whilst you're reading this or about what my daily life as Nomadic FIRE looks like right now, you can look me up on Instagram. You won't find a link to this book or the subjects FYM or FIRE but pictures by me, as a traveler, amateur photographer and expat, of my daily life and my surroundings, wherever on earth I may be.

instagram.com/nomadicmerijn/

For more information about the author:

About the author, Merijn Heijnen
fymfire.com/en/about/

Facebook
The author and the book: from F*ck You Money to FIRE:
facebook.com/From-F_ck-You-Money-to-FIRE-100751668501376/

Instagram
from F*ck You Money to FIRE
instagram.com/from.FuckYouMoney.to.FIRE/